Local history

PAT HUGHES

TEACHER TIMESAVERS

Heritage Park Primary School

Published by Scholastic Ltd,
Villiers House,
Clarendon Avenue,
Leamington Spa,
Warwickshire CV32 5PR

© 1997 Scholastic Ltd

123456789   789012345

Author Pat Hughes
Editor Jane Bishop
Assistant Editor Sally Gray
Series designer Joy White
Designer Louise Belcher
Illustrations Virginia Gray & Andrew Keylock
Cover illustration Frances Lloyd
Cover photograph Martyn Chillmaid

Designed using Aldus Pagemaker
Processed by Pages Bureau, Leamington Spa
Artwork by Steve Williams Design, Leicester
Printed in Great Britain by Ebenezer Baylis & Son, Worcester

British Library Cataloguing-in-Publication Data
A catalogue record for this book is
available from the British Library.

ISBN 0-590-53456-4

Acknowledgements
The author would like to thank the following schools: Prescot CP, Longview CP and Eccleston Lane Ends. The publishers gratefully acknowledge permission to reproduce the following copyright material:
The British Library for permission to redraw maps of Blackpool 1844 and 1897 reproduced by permission of the British Library; Controller of Her Majesty's Stationery Office for outline maps of the UK from the National Curriculum for Geography © Crown copyright 1995; Cowbridge Town Council for permission to produce a drawing of the Cowbridge War Memorial; Croydon Local Studies Library and Archives for a parish Tythe map of Croydon 1847; Kelloggs UK Ltd for the use of the brand name *Kellogg's Corn Flakes* and the use of the name Dr. John Kellogg; Littlewoods Organisation for the permission to redraw from photographs supplied by Littlewoods two Littlewood's shops; Liverpool Record Office for the use of two sections of a map of Liverpool 1846 and 1893; Metropolitan Borough of Knowsley for the use of a map of Prescot in 1592 from *Prescot: A Town Trail;* Ministry of Defence for permission to illustrate three military medals © Crown Copyright/MOD; The National Trust (Fountains Abbey) for permission to reillustrate the plan of Fountains Abbey, Yorkshire; Ordnance Survey for the use of a street map of Chester and one of Dorset and Wiltshire © Crown copyright reserved; Plymouth City Council for permission to depict the tiles on Plymouth Hoe subway; Post Office Education Service for permission to redraw post boxes from a poster supplied by Post Office Education Service; Public Record Office for the map of Carrickfergus 1560 (Ref: MPF 98) © Crown Copyright Public Record Office; Reed Information Services for permission to reproduce two entries from *Kelly's Directories* of 1932 and 1958 for Church Street, Liverpool; Sutton's Seeds Archives for permission to redraw from a 1930s aerial photograph of Sutton's Seeds Reading factory.
Every effort has been made to trace copyright holders and the publishers apologise for any inadvertent omissions.

Contents

About the author

Pat Hughes is a Senior Lecturer in Education at the Liverpool Hope University College and an experienced author of primary history and English books.

Introduction

Local history provides a wealth of opportunities through which to teach the concepts, skills and historical facts outlined in the curriculum documents within a local framework with which children should already be familiar.

The very nature of local history means that the choice of subject matter will be heavily dependent on what has happened in the past in the area near the school and the availability of appropriate source material. This book is a means by which teachers can develop and extend children's skills in using evidence which may be available locally.

Specific objectives

The photocopiable pages in this book aim to:
- develop children's skills in using local history resources such as buildings, archives and photographs;
- help children to interpret the historic environment in their immediate locality by using different sources of evidence;
- provide activities which encourage children to develop their sense of chronology;
- improve children's written recording of local history;
- encourage the use of non-fiction texts to develop historical knowledge and concepts.

Organisation

The first section in the book provides some generic sheets including letters to parents and evaluation sheets. The following eight sections focus on specific sources these are: Maps, The changing landscape, Place-names, Archaeological remains, Buildings, Buildings – remembering and worship, Archives, Pictorial records and Oral history. There are some fact sheets at the beginning of the Buildings section.

Historical skills and concepts

The key historical concepts developed through this approach to local history are chronology, change and evidence.

Children should be using language associated with the passing of time and make comparisons between one period/era and another. Younger children would look at differences between 'then' and 'now' while older children would be involved in looking at continuity between the past and present, discussing similarities as well as differences.

Local history has very practical implications for exploring terms such as heritage. The children will be considering its meaning and the ways in which selected features of the past are preserved for the future.

Key historical skills involve children using a range of local sources to find out about one particular aspect of the past. They need to be able to ask and answer appropriate historical questions related to the aspect they are studying. This involves familiarising themselves with the subject-specific vocabulary as well as the types of questions which elicit the most constructive responses.

Children need to use reference and information-finding skills to seek out answers to their own questions and they will need to be confident in the discovery of uncertainty about many of the answers.

Teachers' Notes

National Curriculum

England and Wales

At Key Stage 1 children should learn about the very recent past of their local community, but they may also learn about particular people and events which have special significance for the area in which they live. These may include people and events from the very distant past. At Key Stage 2 there are three possible approaches to teaching local history:

1. To look at one aspect of the local community and trace its development – or demise – over a long period of time. This could be focused on education, leisure, religion, population change, settlement and landscape, law and order or the treatment of the poor.

2. To find out about one aspect of the local community during a short period of time or to look at the local community's involvement in a particular event. This could provide an opportunity to look at a major event which had important local implications but which is not covered by the National Curriculum until pupils reach secondary school such as the Civil War.

3. To learn about aspects of local history which exemplify another Study Unit which they have already studied or will study in the future. For example buildings or remains of buildings may have survived from the past and provide some evidence about the history of that period. City walls, National Trust or Heritage sites and properties are good examples and may be well resourced for non-specialist history teachers.

Northern Ireland

At Key Stage 1 the draft 1996 Orders acknowledge the likelihood that in the early stages of their education, history is likely to be approached through cross-curricular topics. As children move through the key stage they are more likely to be taught history through history-related topics which focus on a specific period of time or particular people and events.

Aspects of local history can permeate both these approaches. A topic such as school or transport can have a strong local history flavour and topics that focus on a specific period of time such as life in the recent past are also likely to be related closely to the locality. At Key Stage 2 the Orders recommend that local history is taught through one or more of the three Study Units and more specific details are provided in the programmes of study for Life in Early Times, The Vikings and Life in Victorian Times. It is also possible to undertake a local study unrelated to any of the Study Units.

Scotland

Through P1–3 the focus in **Understanding People in the Past** is that pupils develop a sense of the past using their own experience and their immediate environment and its past. This is closely linked to local history. In P4–6 there are several ways in which local historical perspectives can enhance studies of the past taken from the five recommended historical eras.

The photocopiable sheets

The first six pages provide a general section giving guidance for school trips and visits in the locality, letters to parents and individual and class evaluation sheets.

The Geographical Association's publications on field trips are useful to have in school and a school policy on outside visits ensures that visits are seen and treated as an essential part of school life.

Our day out Prior to a visit send parents a letter outlining the purpose of the visit and practical arrangements. Prepare by visiting the proposed site in advance, studying any guide books and educational matter produced on site for the children. List and assess any possible dangers and organisational details as well as teaching and learning points. Be clear exactly what you want the children to get out of the visit and ensure that both they and your helpers understand this. It may be necessary to specify clothing so that children are dressed appropriately and wearing sensible footwear.

Check that you know what is required by law in terms of taking children out of school and that you are familiar with any relevant school and LEA documentation. Seek permission to take children off the school site from the headteacher, governors and parents. Parental consent should be given on a standardised form. Payments cannot be made compulsory so the wording needs to show that this is a voluntary contribution to cover costs. Ensure that school dinner orders have been amended appropriately. Arrange for extra adult help and ensure that they are covered by requirements outlined in the relevant documentation.

If the children will be writing during the visit provide clip-boards and pencils. Ensure that the children know what to wear, what food and drink to bring and how much pocket money will be needed. Check contact numbers and make sure you are aware of any medical requirements; for example inhalers or travel sickness tablets. Ensure that you have a first aid kit, bucket (with or without sand), toilet rolls, paper tissues and air fresheners. A cash float for emergencies is also useful however close the visit is to school.

Our class museum Send a press release to your local paper and/or free paper asking for specific items for the school/class museum, such as carpet beaters, flat irons and hot water bottles. Written sources such as dated local guide books and newspapers can provide an insight into what the local area used to be like at a specific point in time. Photographs of specific events in the past such as visits of local dignitaries can give evidence about clothing and transport and can often be cross-referenced with school log books which record children being taken to see the actual events.

School trip record This will help children to identify the purpose of their visits out of school as well as reminding them of what they saw. They can be added to children's portfolios to show evidence of progression in written recording as well as understanding of historical and geographical concepts.

Making a local history book Use this page as a cover for the children's own books. Local guidebooks and local history pamphlets can provide children with a model for their own writing. Children can record the history of one particular building such as the school, or make a book covering the particular aspect of the local community which the class is studying such as the local football team or local life in the 1950s and 1960s.

Local history personal evaluation sheet This may be filled in with adult support (KS1) and provides a means of helping children to recognise and evaluate their own learning. Encourage the children to provide additional details. For example, older KS1 children may write old/new or then/now by their resource, while KS2 children may be able to give the actual dates of their sources.

Class evaluation sheet Historical skills, concepts and knowledge can be recorded using this sheet which provides a manageable way of recording, but does require supplementing with more general comments on pupils' learning (see previous sheet), together with examples of pupils' work

Maps

Current and historical maps can provide useful source material for finding out about the past in a particular locality. Local libraries, record offices and planning departments are useful starting points. Local history books aimed at the adult market often contain maps which can be adapted for young children. In school you need to have several copies of different types of maps for children to work on. Try to ensure that the geographical skills needed for interpreting maps are matched with work on mapping being undertaken in geography.

School plans: now and then The plans on the sheet show a very simple change to a nursery unit. Ask the children why they think this change has been made and what other changes might be found in different areas of the nursery. Encourage the children to look at their own classroom: is there any evidence that the room has been changed since it was built? Can they suggest ways in which it might be changed in the future for example if more/less children were admitted/if it was extended/if all children had their own computer.

Street scene *Answers*: the tourist map of Chester provided shows that the castle is now used as a Military Museum. Streets with religious names include White Friars, Nun's Road, Werburgh Street and Trinity Street. Trade streets include Weaver Street, Hunter Street and Pepper Street. The Roman amphitheatre covered a wide area and was used as a circus, bull-ring and training ground for the army. Games and public punishments were also held there. Space was at a premium within the city walls, so the amphitheatre was placed outside. Some children may need help with the abbreviations used on the map such as ST. (street), St. (saint), H.Q. (headquarters), SQ. (square), P (Car park). Can the children provide a key for the map to help other users?

Mapping remains Ordnance Survey maps show ancient tracts and remains. This sheet shows how a map can be made from these remains to give some indication of settlement at one particular point in history.

Roman Britain *Answers*: One fort, three temples and shrines, five villas. Other evidence on the map provided are place-names, roads, rivers and physical setting for sites.

Changing cities *Answers*: same names – Chapel Street, Dale Street, Castle Street; changed names – Juggler Street to High Street, Bank Street to Water Street and Moor Street to Tithebarn Street.

Living towns *Answer*: Kragfargvs Towne.

Local industry Occupations for the people would have included – farmers, labourers, potters, priest and millers. The stocks and ducking stool were used as punishments in Tudor times.

Growth of a city There are 47 years between the maps. Streets which are on both maps are: Church Street, Everton Terrace, St. George's, Lowry Street and Waterhouse Lane. Streets which have been added are: Copeland, Stonewall, Hibbert, Abbey, Druid and Jefferson. The maps provide evidence of the large number of dwellings built to accommodate people moving into the city.

Growth of a seaside town The railways made it possible for people to get out of the towns to visit seaside resorts such as Blackpool. The second map shows how Blackpool grew to accommodate this. The map shows evidence of additional houses as well as three piers, a lifeboat station, Blackpool Tower and railway lines and station. Cheaper property would have been built to accommodate the people who worked in hotels, boarding houses and shops.

Tithe maps Tithe maps were made by the parish to show how much land different individuals owned and included details such as ponds, the types of fields and other land. One tenth of the annual produce of the land or labour was taken by the church as a tax. Tithe barns were built to store the tithes which were paid in kind. Dwelling houses marked on this map are College Water Farm, Norwoodbury Lodge, Ellen's Villa, Beulah Cottage, White Horse Farm and White Horse Cottage.

The changing landscape

Let the children look at the landscape around the school and suggest ways in which it may have changed over the years. The sheets in this section show children how simple changes in people's lives influence the landscape. Other sheets in this section are designed to encourage children to think about how leisure, entertainment, transport and shopping have all influenced the landscape. The final section indicates that landscape changes are not always welcomed. Discuss ways in which the past is preserved locally and the influence this may have on the landscape. This could include increased traffic on the roads, changes in the skyline caused by 'attractions' such as fairgrounds, car and coach parks, litter and pollution.

Early settlements Encourage the children to look at the landscape features in the illustration and to consider which would be attractive to early settlers. Settlements tended to be close to a water source, and near forests so that fuel did not have to be carried far. Traditional tracts meant that people could travel from one area to another, although most people would stay in their own communities most of their lives.

Farming Commercial pig farmers use modern technology for cost effectiveness. Pigs are kept inside, so buildings are required and food must be brought to them and waste matter extracted from the buildings. Pig farms can be very smelly, so they may be set back from other dwellings. Acknowledge the increased number of vegetarians in the community and be sensitive to children who have strong views for and against the farming of animals for slaughter in any discussion.

A new theme Encourage the children to consider parks which they know of. Provide a collection of tourist brochures as an initial stimulus and support for children who haven't visited a theme park. Ask children to consider the meaning of heritage buildings and sites if they need the commercial support of theme parks. How do they feel about reconstructed history? Should only original material be shown or do role-plays and reconstructions help to make the past seem more interesting? Do they think this could confuse very young children by mixing fact with fiction.

Sport and entertainment Let children work in small groups with an adult to discuss this sheet. Link the activity closely with sports and entertainment facilities in your area with which the children are familiar. Encourage the children to look at the different physical changes in the landscape caused by each of these amenities as well as changes to ensure access (roads, carparks, seating, floodlighting and security).

Transport Children in schools near airports, railways and ports could extend the activity to look in greater detail at landscape changes caused by the different forms of transport.

Shopping The gradual change in shopping shown is caused largely by an increase in money, leisure time and car ownership. Early settlements involved much subsistence farming with the surplus taken and sold in the local market town. As people moved into more specialised employment they used money to buy the food surplus which other people had created. Specialist shops were established to sell specific products – bread, fruit and vegetables, meat. With the advent of today's retail parks many urban children will be familiar with the idea of spending leisure time 'shopping'.

No! No! No! The children's answers will depend on what is happening in their own area. The land could be used for: housing, a retail shopping park or a sports centre, for example. Ask the children whether they would be more concerned about some land usages than others for example a sports centre or a housing development.

Place-names

Many place-names have grown over time, so that an Anglo-Saxon word may have been added to a Celtic word to create a place-name. The Scandinavian invasion and settlement which took place during the 9th, 10th and 11th centuries resulted in many place-names of Scandinavian origin to the North and East of England. By the time the Normans arrived most settlements and landscape features already had established names. French names were given to the newly built castles, estates and monasteries – Battle and Belvoir for example. French-speaking families often added their names to their manors. This resulted in many double-barrelled names, for example Sutton Courtenay, Stanton Lacy. More generally place names can be divided into three main groups – folk names, habitative names and topographical names. Folk names are derived from the original inhabitants of the area. Essex and Sussex are both old Anglo-Saxon kingdoms for example. Habitative names show places which have been inhabited from very early times. So the place-name describes a particular kind of habitation for example: homesteads, farms, enclosures, villages, cottages and other kinds of buildings and settlements. Topographical names originally consisted of a description of some topographical or physical feature – natural or made by humans. This name was then transferred to any settlement near the landscape feature named. The names for rivers, streams, fords, roads, marshes and moors, hills and valleys are often found in place-names.

What's in a name? *Answers*: Knight, Fisher.

Collecting words Encourage children to look at the environmental print around them to find clues about the past. Examples of both warning signs and historic signs are given on the sheet. This page could be used as a homework activity, with an adult helping.

Street names Children may need help with abbreviations used for local street names for example St. Rd. Cres. Origins of older street names can be investigated using this sheet but children living in newer housing estates may also look for reasons for their street names.

Guess the street names Look at some local maps to find some appropriate street names.

Travelling names Halifax – Canada; Boston – North America; Melbourne – Australia; Plymouth – North America; South Wales – Australia; Newcastle – Australia.

Celtic place-names Dungannon – fort; Kilkenny – chapel; Aberdeen – the mouth of a river; Caernarfon – fort; Ilfracombe – valley.

A Roman legacy Children might find Chester, Ribchester, Gloucester, Colchester, Manchester, Newcastle, Lancaster, Portchester. More able children could use reference books to find out more about Roman forts, villas and towns.

An Anglo-Saxon legacy Older children could use a dictionary of place-names to check their evidence, since there is an element of uncertainty about the origins of many place-names.

Did the Vikings settle near your school? Children who have studied the Vikings may be able to show how and why Viking place-names are restricted to one area of the country.

Norman place-names By 1066 most settlements had established names. Norman place-names tended to be given when a Norman family built and settled in an area. Check for local examples.

Archaeological remains

Archaeology is all about building up a picture of how people lived in the past from the clues that they left behind. Encourage children to develop their skills of interpretation through working systematically on artefacts which will involve them in observation, recording and analysis.

Movable remains *Answers:* Roman coins, jewellery, lead curse. Some of the objects may have been lost in the drain while people were bathing and there is evidence that some were thrown into sacred water as gifts for the gods. Children in Scotland or Northern Ireland will have no local Roman finds, so concentrate on why not

and on what Celtic remains exist instead. Celtic remains have also been found in lakes. It is likely that Romans adopted this practice from them.

Artefacts in local museums Encourage children to use their imagination about what an object would have looked like when it was in use. Arrange to visit the museum in advance to provide support with suitable non-fiction texts and postcards if available, prior to the children visiting the museum.

How did it get there? Looking at the illustrations of an Egyptian mummy, a Roman statue, a Greek pot and an African mask, the children may find out that all of these objects are likely to have been stolen or taken from other countries. Initially they may have been part of one person's collection.

Making a class museum These sheets look at ways in which archaeologists investigate unknown objects in a systematic manner. They start by creating a database which describes and suggests possible uses for the object. Link this area of investigative historical inquiry with science and/or technology understanding. Encourage children to use non-fiction texts, particularly photographs and illustrations, to help them identify objects.

History at breakfast This provides an opportunity to look at history as evidence in household names. Children could investigate the history of other everyday items such as the Hoover, Biro and sandwich. Here the name provides the initial source of evidence.

Buildings

Buildings are the most obvious remains in any locality for primary children to observe and analyse and so this forms the largest section of the book, starting with fact sheets to help children to classify different aspects of buildings

in their locality. The fifth fact sheet looks at local styles of buildings characteristic of different areas of the country.

Building materials fact sheet Different types of stonework and brickwork are illustrated to help children identify the different types of construction used in their area.

Roofing fact sheet Some children may not have seen a thatched roof, yet they exist in many areas. The thatch itself is usually reed or straw. Reed thatch lasts much longer than straw. Slates were originally used only on houses near quarries because of the expense of transporting them. Look too at chimney pots; most new housing is built without chimneys and many older houses have had their chimneys removed.

Doors fact sheet/ Windows fact sheet These illustrations will help children to identify different doors/windows in their own neighbourhood. If there is a rich variety of doors/windows from different periods children can use observational drawings to make a timeline for the area.

Local building styles fact sheet Identifies traditional building styles built in specific areas. In clay soil areas of the country, bricks could be made cheaply so were used widely there.

Reading buildings – questions to ask Suggests points which can be investigated to find out more about a particular building. The relevant fact sheets can be used to provide specialised information for more able children.

Local architectural features This encourages children to develop their knowledge of words used to describe features of a building. Children's observational skills can also be increased.

Historic buildings – ancient Egypt Looks at the legacy provided by the Egyptians to our own buildings and more specifically at buildings in the local area.

Historic buildings – ancient Greece Looks at three different types of Greek columns known as 'orders'. These are found in many public buildings and children can be encouraged to identify them. Many buildings contain more than one sort of column. Children can discuss when these buildings were constructed and why and how they were influenced by architectural features from ancient Greece.

Historic designs – domes Some local areas have very few domes, whereas others have several. Once children have investigated the domes in their community they should be able to say from where the architectural influence has come.

Why settle here? This sheet links well with work in geography about localities and the reasons for settlement. This activity is likely to be more successful and constructive with children whose local area is well established. However, urban sprawls also have a history and often oral histories can be used very successfully to show why people have moved out of cities.

The changing story of a settlement The pictures show how a settlement can change over time. Let children work in a small group with an adult to look at reasons for these changes.

Village buildings Many villages were established as a particular type of settlement. Newer buildings may have disguised this, but children could consider whether they think their village was originally linear in shape; cross-shaped; following the flow of a river or the sea; fitting into a gap in the hills or was a settlement round a castle or abbey.

Village survey Villages often have several features in common. The church or chapel is often the defining point for what makes a hamlet into a village. Many villages have village greens,

a post office, perhaps a school and usually a public house. Some villages are display villages and actively encourage tourists.

Changing cities Keep this as an open-ended activity so that children can describe several things which could have happened to this city.

Winds and local history Towns and cities which grew up during the industrial revolution are good examples of how town development took place in the interests of the factory owners. They built their own houses downhill from the pollution created by their factories, while their workers lived and worked close to the factory. Let children discuss how their town has changed from this pattern of development.

Places of safety and defence Children living close to a fort, dyke or castle could also note some of the reasons why their area needed such a defence.

Defending the coastline The Romans built forts and warning stations against the invading Saxons. Later, beacons were erected to warn of invasion. The Normans built castles, although like the Irish round houses (built as protection against the Vikings) these are not always on the coast. Henry VIII built artillery forts and Martello towers were built at the end of the eighteenth century and beginning of the nineteenth against French invasion. Pill boxes were built during the Second World War for much the same reason. The sheet asks children to match the defence to the period and order into a timeline. More able readers could find out more about the specific purposes for building them. Children living in established towns could look for evidence of town defence such as town gateways and walls.

Under attack Castles can be found in most parts of the country, most of them were built by the Normans after 1066. This sheet shows a very

simple motte and bailey castle which was one of the earliest built. It consisted of a wooden fort on the top of a hill or mound and a fence enclosing an area known as the bailey. The hills or mottes can sometimes be seen, although the wooden structures have long since disappeared. When the Normans were better established they built castles of stone, with a central keep surrounded by battlements. Children could also examine from whom the Normans were defending themselves.

Parts of a castle This is a fairly traditional design, but children living in Scotland may be more familiar with Scottish baronial castles which have a very distinctive architectural style. In several parts of England and Wales fortified manor houses still exist from the fourteenth and fifteenth centuries. Some of these were surrounded by moats.

Spot the difference – houses This is a much less demanding activity, children are asked to look for changes which take place in the appearance of homes over a period of time. Children's understanding of the historical concept of change can be identified through the type of responses to the question about why they think the changes have happened. If there are any Victorian houses in the local area this sheet could be used in conjunction with them.

Inside homes This extends the previous activity and looks at the inside of a house which is over 150 years old. Children can make comparisons between their own home and the one in the illustration and if possible identify old houses and cottages in their area which may have been altered to accommodate modern conveniences such as central heating and electricity.

Visiting an old cottage Some of the most effective evidence for how rural areas once looked comes from aerial photographs. Open-air museums have used this evidence as well as oral and written evidence to reconstruct small villages. Sometimes a whole house or cottage has been transferred to the museum. The plan can be used to collect evidence about what life was like for people who lived in a cottage without running water and with an outside toilet.

The history of my home This activity encourages children to look at their own homes as a historical piece of evidence. Even very new housing has often been changed from its original design and children may remember ways in which the structure of the house has been altered since they moved in.

Changing homes Let children look at housing in their own locality and identify houses that were built at different times and make a simple timeline of local housing. Make sure that children living in older property are not made to feel that this is in any way inferior to living in a much newer house. As an extension ask the children to look at the houses nearby and to find three built at different times. They could sketch them and make a local housing timeline.

Visiting a stately home This covers visits to stately homes and suggests one way in which children can record their visit systematically. A visit like this can be used to show ways in which people lived in the past. Television programmes have made children very aware of the differences between those living upstairs and those 'below stairs' in such houses.

Gardens and grounds Ideally children should have the opportunity to smell and taste different herbs which might have been grown in the past in their area. They can look at different ways in which herbs were used such as flavouring for food, medicines and disguising bad smells.

Spot the difference – school Children can consider ways in which their school building has changed over the years. Encourage them to suggest reasons why the building has changed.

Investigating change in your school This provides a detailed investigation sheet for looking at changes in the school and identifying different signs within the school building which record the school's history.

Investigating changes inside your school This is an extension of the previous sheet to highlight other areas for children to investigate changes within their school building more closely.

Investigating changes outside your school Use the fact sheets on pages 56–59 to look at changes which have occurred on the outside of school buildings.

School log books Younger children will need to have extracts from the log book read to them, but all the children should have the opportunity to see the school log book.

School log book investigation This provides a suggested check list of things which children could investigate using the log book as a primary source of evidence. Old log books in particular can provide very useful and interesting information.

Punishment book These are not as easy to find as log books, but when available provide an interesting insight into the types of punishment given to children in the past and the reasons for it. Comparisons between now and then can also be made.

Signs of the trade This sheet moves children out of the school into the local community to look at different shop signs. At a time when many people could not read, shop signs were an important way in which wares could be advertised and the shops selling them identified.

Inn signs – fact sheet Old inn signs can provide useful clues to the age and origin of a building as well as recording a special local history. The fact sheet provides background information for children to investigate local inn signs.

Inn signs Investigating local inn signs is a good opportunity for children who are starting to read to look at environmental print and symbols.

Shopping This examines changes in one particular shop and children can be encouraged to look for changes in shops in their own areas. Old photographs and illustrations can be used and local newspapers are often helpful in providing relevant archive material.

Local industry map The map shows industry at a very early point in the nineteenth century. The stable industry was agriculture and this particular local map shows the continued importance of salt production in Northwich, Nantwich and Middlewich. Textiles were assuming importance in Congleton, Macclesfield and north-east Cheshire. Show children local maps indicating the types of industry in place in their area before and after the Victorian era.

Factory site This factory was initially set up in Victorian times to deal in corn and agricultural seeds. The Victorians were interested in gardening and gradually the factory began to move into manufacturing flower and vegetable seeds. By the 1930s this was the bulk of its business. The size of each building gives an idea of the importance of the department to which it belonged. The Firemen's cottages on site indicate the fire hazard involved. The relatively small garage indicates that the bulk of transportation was done by rail, rather than road. Factory owners often built and rented out cheap accommodation for their work force. In some areas these can provide useful evidence about local industry. Weavers' and clock makers' cottages often had a long window on their upper floor to throw light on to their work in attic bedrooms. Miners' cottages were often built near the mines they worked. The older the factory the easier it is to recognise the type of industry from its buildings.

Waterways The majority of canals were dug between 1760 and 1830 and were an important form of transport until the railways took over the bulk of their trade. Today they are often used by pleasure boats, but there is plenty of historical evidence about their past from artefacts and buildings running alongside the canal – such as lock keepers' cottages, inn signs, toll houses and tow paths.

Railways The maps indicate the rise of the railway system in the UK and give some idea of the landscape changes they created when they were built. In several areas disused lines have been made into walkways and railway cottages and stations transferred to other uses. Notices are often left as relics of the railway age and carry the imprint of an old railway company. Street names, railway inns and hotels are all evidence of railways.

I-spy historic roads Even in prehistoric times there were trackways and old ways show the existence of these. The Romans built roads which have continued to exist. In the eighteenth century turnpike trusts were built and these are indicated today by the presence of toll bars and toll houses. Signposts, milestones, boundary stones, wayside crosses and monuments may all be found by roads and provide evidence of different periods in the past.

Streets This is a very simple sheet designed to develop children's awareness in differences between then and now.

Street furniture This sheet shows some examples of street furniture which children could look for in their area. Older pupils could investigate the original reasons for these relics. Cobblestones still give a better grip in icy weather!

Royal Mail Edward VIII abdicated before his Coronation, so very few post-boxes show his initials. Make and display a stamp timeline alongside the post-box timeline.

I-spy street lights Lamp-posts are a good example of changing fashions. Replica gas lamps appear in some areas to create an olde-world atmosphere.

Street entertainment Entertainers are sometimes employed directly by the local authority to encourage people into an area. In large cities street entertainment often takes the form of busking and is more like that of a century ago. In some areas there are special streets set aside as play streets, but for the majority of children, today's streets are no longer places in which they can play.

Skeleton of a community Ideally children should work with photographs of some of the major buildings in their own community. This sheet is intended to raise awareness of local facilities as well as to identify major buildings in the community which have their own individual histories.

Recording evidence of change This sheet asks the children to focus in on one particular building and can be used by several children in the class to gradually build up a data base on the history of local buildings.

A new lease of life Some buildings may have gone through several changes – warehouses and cinemas for example. Encourage children to look for evidence of their previous purpose.

Buildings – remembering and worship

Plaques on buildings Use a school plaque as a starting point. Datestones on buildings sometimes need to be treated with caution because the stone may have been moved from another building or the date might simply mark an extension to the main building.

Memorials The tiles at Plymouth not only provide a timeline of major events in English history but also show the importance of Plymouth in the making of this history. Some local memorials may not have a plaque but may be named after someone who has given land or money. There are some very exciting and artistically creative ways in which past history is recorded today such as stained glass windows, tapestries and statues. Encourage children to find ways in which the past has been recorded in their own neighbourhood.

Monuments in time These are just four monuments which provide evidence of people and events in the past. Children could create their own monuments guide for the area in which they live.

A place to worship Recognising the variety of places in which people worship is an important element in children's spiritual development (including children whose families don't take part in formal ceremonies). The children may find out that sometimes buildings have undergone extensive conversion from their original purposes.

War memorials These exist all over the country and when examined may tell us a lot about weapons and uniform in the past. Memorials in the form of brasses and effigies are often found in churches.

A Sikh gurdwara It is particularly important that children who do not live in multi-faith communities gain some understanding of different ways and places of worship. Teachers in multi-faith schools may wish to cover the labels and ask children to fill them in themselves. The most famous gurdwara is the Golden Temple at Amristar in the Punjab in India.

A mosque Children who have limited experience of other faiths can use this as a starting point to find out more about Islam and its history through historical research.

Changing churches The sheet shows a growing building as populations grew and more emphasis was placed on the importance of going to church. Today, the reverse is happening and in many areas churches have fallen into decay. Some churches and church buildings may get a new lease of life as furniture warehouses, restaurants or private nurseries.

Church check list Local churches often have a rich history and may produce small guidebooks outlining this. Churches can be classified by age, building materials used, their shape or their religious denomination.

Village church Comparisons can be made between different churches and also between worship amongst different faiths. Many churches sell small books about the history of the building often containing a plan. Visit your local church, make a plan of it and compare it to the plan in the guide book. Write a short guide book to the church for young children who have never visited a church before.

Church furniture Identifying the purpose of church furniture as well as its existence is important in understanding the history behind church rituals which may be very important to people in the community.

Chapels Not all church-goers chose such formal surroundings. Local chapels and halls may have a much simpler design and pupils can make comparisons between these and the more formal church features. Children who have studied the Tudor era may be able to make links between what happened during and after the Reformation and what exists today.

Using plans Plans like this often appear in guide books and this sheet provides an opportunity to learn how to 'read' a plan. Studying a plan beforehand can be the first step in interpretation of a site. Illustrations and photographs of reconstructed sites are also useful.

Roman numerals fact sheet Encourage children to identify Roman numerals in their everyday lives, for example some television programmes end with the full date in Roman numerals.

Graveyards – fact sheet Work on gravestones can be used as an opportunity to teach children how a graveyard should be respected as well as a reminder of our own mortality, and can be a rich source of information.

Unusual epitaphs Today these are often found in local newspapers, but local gravestones may reveal a few gems. Gravestones are usually single slabs of stone, but early ones may take the form of 'table tombs'. The oldest gravestones will probably date from the eighteenth century and some of these may have verses as well as names and dates.

Reading gravestones Very old gravestones are difficult to read, but sometimes there are local records with typed versions. Victorian gravestones can reveal a great deal about the life as well as the death of a community and children are usually horrified by the huge child mortality rate an investigation reveals. Written source material from church registers can also be used to supplement evidence from local churchyards. Gravestones can be used to find evidence about local families as well as local trades and occupations.

Archives

The census A population census has been taken every ten years since the beginning of the nineteenth century. Forms are distributed to and collected from each household and the details copied into books which are kept in the Public Record Office in London. The information has now been transferred onto microfilm or microfiche and this is available in archive offices and many local libraries.

Census research This sheet covers census details for a couple of households. Ideally children should use census returns for streets near their own school so that they can see the actual houses in which the people lived. This census form comes from Liverpool and the terraced houses still exist.

Census returns All personal information in the census remains confidential for 100 years and until 1841 only the numbers of people in various categories were recorded that is, no names or personal details. From 1851 exact ages were asked for. Six dates are available 1841–1891. This is a simpler sheet with details of one household.

Church records The church warden was responsible for keeping the church in good repair and the accounts record the cost of this. This sheet also shows some of the other people who were involved in the upkeep of the church. Church bells were often an expensive item and since they were used so much they needed constant attention. Ringers were often given beer as well as money because ringing was thirsty work.

Church registers Henry VIII required all priests to keep a record of births, marriages and deaths. Gradually different registers were used for each event. The sheet shows an extract from a death register which has been transcribed by a local history group in alphabetical, rather than in chronological order. Original registers are usually found in county record offices and many counties have had some published in printed form – particularly marriage registers. Modern registers remain where the event took place.

Inventories These listed a person's belongings and date from the Tudor and Stuart era. They were done by four 'honest persons', usually neighbours of the deceased. Local history books dealing with the Tudor and Stuart era often contain examples of inventories which have been transcribed as do some guidebooks for National Trust properties.

Political pamphlets This sheet enables children to interpret data from evidence collected in the last century. There was a great deal of concern about the living conditions of the poor and this data was collected to show the extent of poverty in one particular ward.

Local newspapers Local newspapers can shed an interesting light on daily life as well as important local events at a particular period. Encourage children to look for local news, advertisements and information notices. Local newspapers can be found in local libraries and some hold older copies on microfilm.

Street directory These were first produced in the nineteenth century to provide exact information of names and addresses for the benefit of the Post Office to ensure that letters were delivered correctly. They differed from earlier more commercial directories which often only contained the wealthy households.

Street plan This develops children's skills in using written source materials by looking at extracts from two street directories and using the information. The very early directories published in the eighteenth and early nineteenth century often contained detailed information; a local historical society may have transcribed these into a more accessible format.

Pictorial records

Photographs are one of the most important sources of information about the past locally. Building up a good resource bank can be relatively inexpensive if children and adults working in the school are asked for photographs and these are classified and copied. Draw children's attention to the possible bias in many photographs and they will learn to spot obviously posed photographs. Children need to ask why the photograph was taken as well as how and when it was shot. Photographs taken of the local area over a period of time can be used for sequencing as well as looking at specific aspects of life in the past.

Picture prompts Photographs are a particularly useful resource for developing the children's concept of change and this sheet suggests one way in which this can be recorded, either by the children themselves or by an adult working closely with them.

Interpreting photographs This sheet aims to develop skills in interpretation, so that children become more aware of the need to evaluate the veracity of evidence placed before them. Extend this activity with the children when they take photographs themselves by asking them to consider the demands they themselves often place on other people when they want to take a 'good' photograph.

Above ground clues – fact sheet This alerts children to ways in which former settlements and developments can be identified long after they have ceased to exist.

Oral history

Oral history means spoken accounts of events and experiences and covers both the past and present. Local museums and history societies may keep taped recordings and supplement these with photographs and written records.

Memories: which is which? This supports children in understanding and interpreting different sorts of evidence. They can discuss whether one source is more reliable than another and the need to check different oral histories against each other.

Badges *Answers:* The first three medals are from the Second World War, the fourth is from the Falklands War and the fifth is from the Gulf War. Asking for stories behind particular artefacts enables children to gather evidence in a more familiar narrative context.

Farming interview Children sometimes have difficulty conducting interviews and it helps to practise in pairs in the classroom before interviews take place. Allowing the interviewee time to expand on the initial question is often a problem. It is also difficult to avoid very long digressions.

Oral evidence: school in the past After children have collected their evidence, they could work in groups organised by decades. They could then present their evidence to the class in terms of 'schools in the 1960s'.

General interview This schedule enables children to suggest their own questions and should be followed up by looking at the type of response gained from specific questions.

Our day out

Dear Parents,

As part of our local history project we are planning to take the class on

a trip to _____

The trip will take place on _____

The children will leave school at _____ and will return by _____

The cost of the trip will be _____

The children will need to bring/wear _____

Pocket money will/will not be needed.

Please sign the form below to give us your permission to take your child on this educational trip. The form should be returned to school as soon as possible together with a voluntary contribution of £............ which would be appreciated to cover the cost.

Yours sincerely,

✂ -

I give permission for (child's name) ....

in (class) .... to attend the school trip to ....

on.............. and enclose £..............

Signed ....

Our class museum

Our class museum

This term ....school is doing a local history project.

As part of this we would like to set up a class museum on the theme of

_____

We would like to include items such as _____

_____

If you have any items or photographs on this subject which you could lend us for our museum we would be very grateful. Children will be looking at and touching the objects in the museum display, so they will need to be fairly robust.

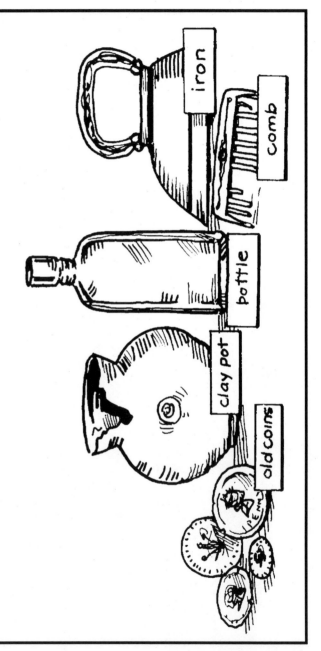

iron

comb

bottle

clay pot

old coins

School trip record

Name: _____

We visited (name of place): _____

On: _____

We left school at: _____

And returned to school at: _____

We were at _____ for (time spent): _____

We went there to: _____

Distance: _____

Time of journey: _____

What I saw: _____
_____

What I did: _____
_____

What I enjoyed most: _____
_____

Name _____

Making a local history book

Making a local history book

Local history books are very personal. People put in them what they think is important about the place in which they live. Sometimes they are all about buildings and places, sometimes people. This picture can be photocopied and used as a front cover for your own local guide book. If you want to make a larger book, ask your teacher to enlarge this on a photocopier.

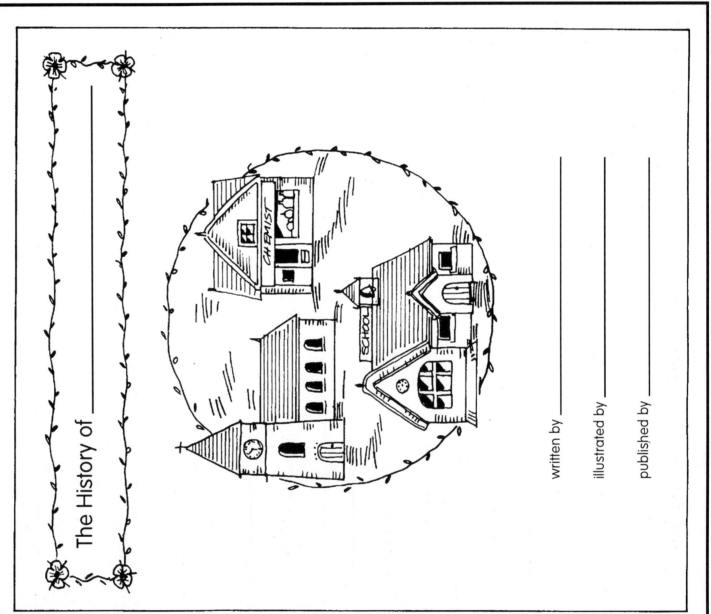

The History of _____

written by _____

illustrated by _____

published by _____

Local history personal evaluation sheet

Local history personal evaluation sheet

1. What I have learned about local history this term: _____

2. What I have enjoyed most about the topic: _____

3. Books I have used to find out about local history: _____

4. Writing I have carried out for the topic: _____

Resources used for local history	✓	example
Maps		
Artefacts		
Photographs		
Written records from the past		
Information from a trip		
Buildings/monuments		
Local people		
Photocopiable sheets		

Name _____

Class evaluation sheet

Children's names

Class evaluation sheet

	1. (a) Distinguishes between present and past.	(b) Can sequence a few local events.	(c) Can sequence a few objects.	(d) Uses simple terms about passing of time.	(e) Retells a story from the past.	(f) Can use simple sources of information about the area such as a photograph.	2. (a) Knowledge about two past events in the area.	(b) Knowledge about two people who used to live in the area.	(c) Responds to information about the past relating to these people and events.	(d) Asks basic historical questions.	(e) Can describe obvious differences between the past and present from local photographs.

Children's names

Class evaluation sheet

	3. (a) Recognises different periods in the past.	(b) Can use relevant dates.	(c) Recognises similarities and differences with today.	(d) Makes simple deductions about events.	(e) Knows which books supply suitable information.	4. (a) Can list main points from source material used.	(b) Utilises information about other historical periods covered.	(c) Makes simple imaginative reconstructions of locality in the past.	5. (a) Can provide individual account of life in the past.	(b) Can support account with historical evidence from variety of sources.

Name _____

School plans: now and then

School plans: now and then

Here is a plan of a nursery in 1992.

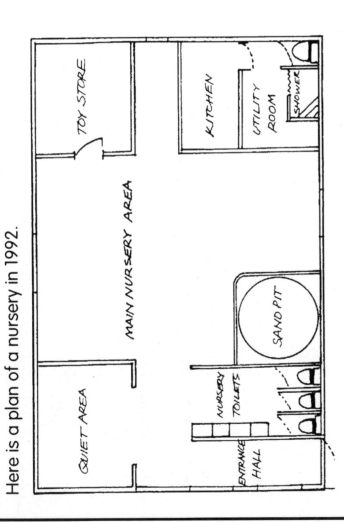

Here is a plan of the same nursery today.

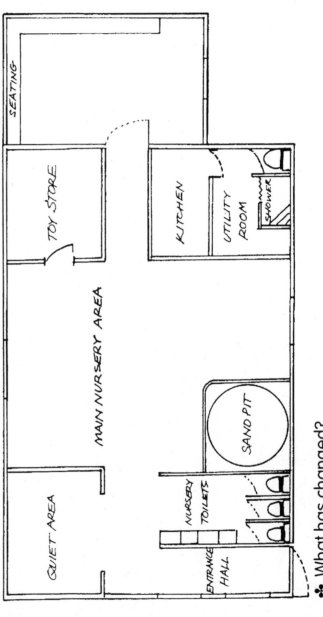

✤ What has changed?

✤ Why do you think it has changed?

✤ Draw a plan of your classroom today. Then draw a plan of your classroom as it might look in 10 years time. You could sketch your ideas on the back of this sheet.

Name _____

Street scene

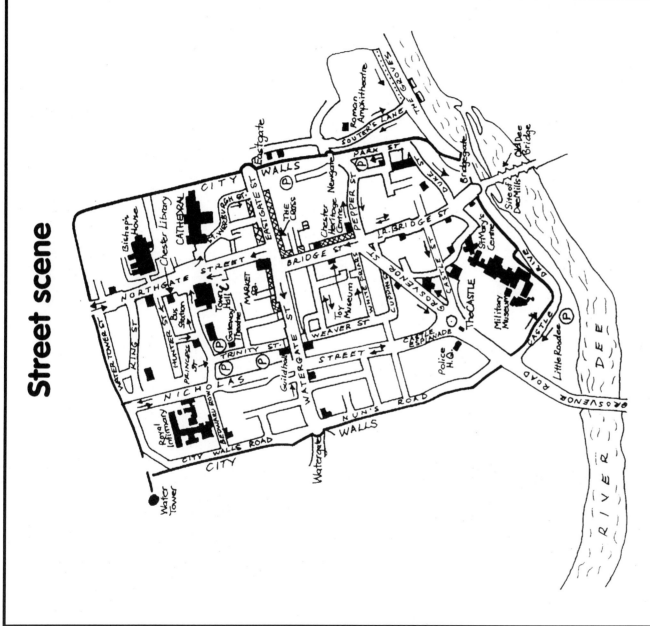

❖ What is the castle used for today?

❖ Write down two streets which have a religious name.

❖ Write down two streets named after a craft or trade.

❖ Why is the Roman amphitheatre outside the city walls?

❖ What do the street names here tell you about the history of Chester?

❖ Look at some street names near your school. What do these names tell you about your neighbourhood?

Name ____________

Mapping remains

Roman Britain

✤ Use a reference book about the Romans to find the modern names for these towns.

Antonine wall
Hadrians Wall
Eburacum
Mamucium
Lindum
Deva
Ratae Coritanorum
Segontium
Viroconium
Ermine Street
Watling Street
Fosse Way
Isca Silurum
Verulamium
Aquae Sulis
Londinium
Isca Dumnoniorum

✤ What other information does this map provide about Roman remains in Britain?

✤ Which was the nearest Roman town to your school? Mark it on the map.

✤ What other historical evidence is there for Roman settlement in this town?

✤ Why is there little evidence of Roman settlement in Scotland, Wales and Ireland on this map?

Name _____

Roman Britain

Ordnance Survey maps show ancient tracts and ancient remains such as hill forts, iron-age settlements and Roman remains. Historians and geographers have worked together to produce maps for specific periods in time. Here is an extract from a map showing Roman remains in the Dorset-Wiltshire area.

How many:

 forts?

 temples and shrines?

 villas?

✤ What other information does this map provide?

✤ Use an Ordnance Survey map of your area to see if there are any historical remains marked. Make a list of them on the back of this sheet. See if you can find out any more information about them.

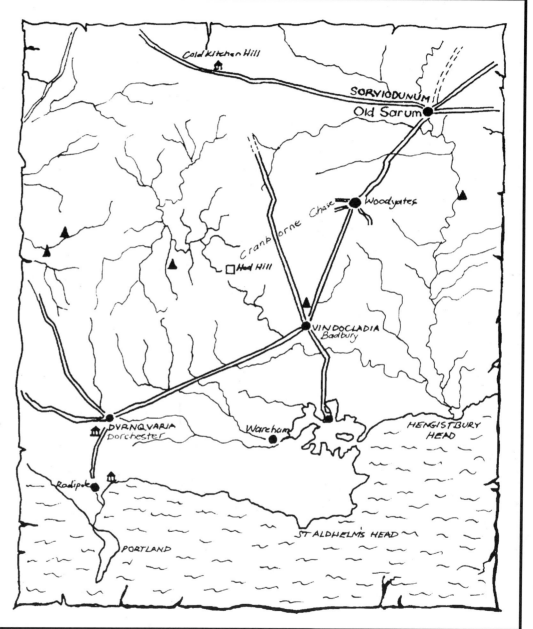

Name _____

Changing cities

This plan shows the city of Liverpool in 1485.

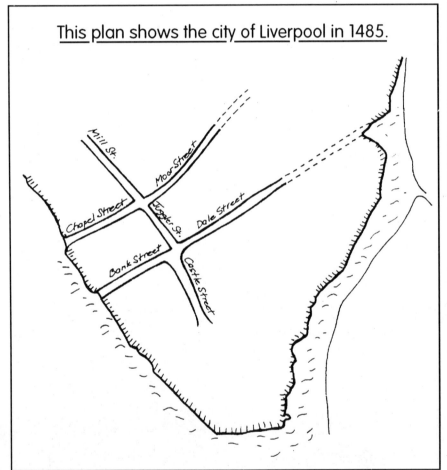

This plan shows the same city 200 years later in 1660.

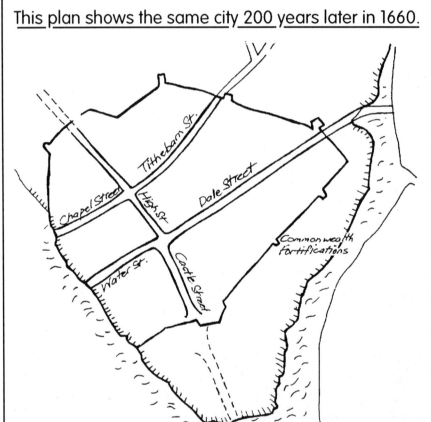

♣ Which streets have the same names?

♣ Which streets have changed their names?

♣ Use an old plan of a city, town or village near your school to make a list of some of the street names and buildings which have disappeared.

Living towns

✤ Write down the name of the town in Tudor English.

✤ Label the castle, church, friary and village cross.

✤ Use non-fiction books about life in Tudor times to draw a picture of the inside of one of the bee-hive huts.

✤ Use a book showing maps made in the fifteenth or sixteenth centuries to find a Tudor plan of your nearest town.

Carrickfergus, County Antrim 1560

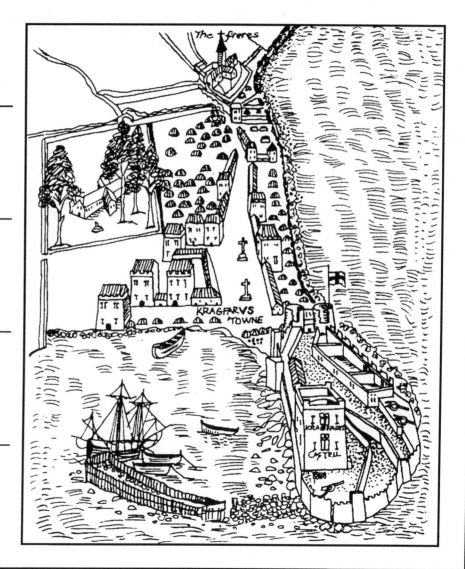

Local industry

Local industry

Here is a map of a small town in 1592.

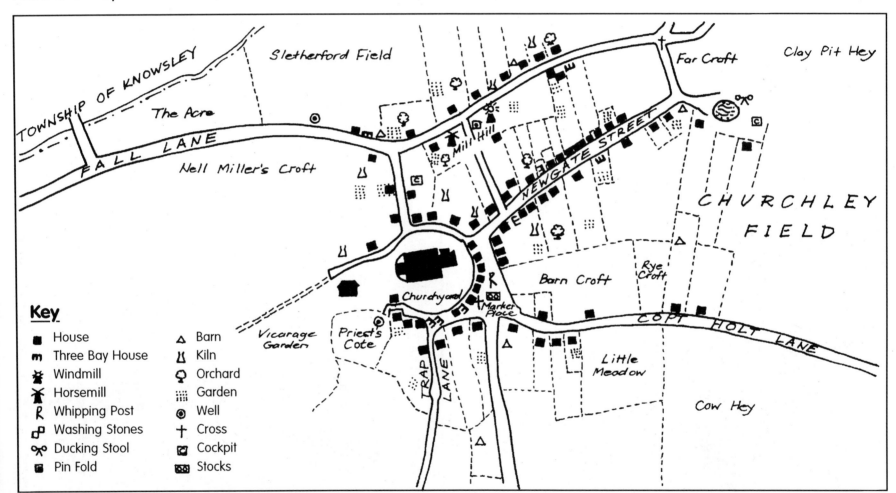

Key

- ■ House
- ʍ Three Bay House
- ✻ Windmill
- ✖ Horsemill
- ʀ Whipping Post
- ⌗ Washing Stones
- ✂ Ducking Stool
- ▣ Pin Fold

- △ Barn
- ⋓ Kiln
- ♀ Orchard
- ⣿ Garden
- ◉ Well
- ✝ Cross
- ▤ Cockpit
- ▦ Stocks

♣ What evidence does this map give about local occupations and how people were punished?

Growth of a city

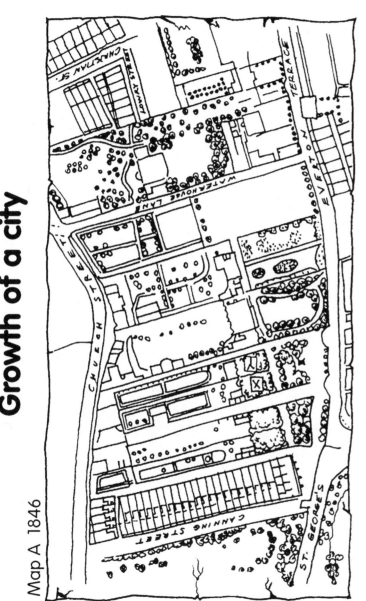

Map A 1846

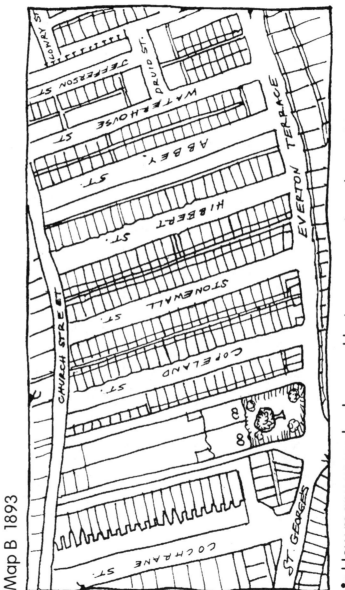

Map B 1893

❖ How many years had passed between map A and map B?

❖ Which streets are on both maps and which have been added?

❖ What information do these maps give you about what was happening in this area during Victorian times?

❖ What was happening at the same time in the nearest city to your school?

Name _____

Growth of a seaside town

Growth of a seaside town

Map of Blackpool published in 1844

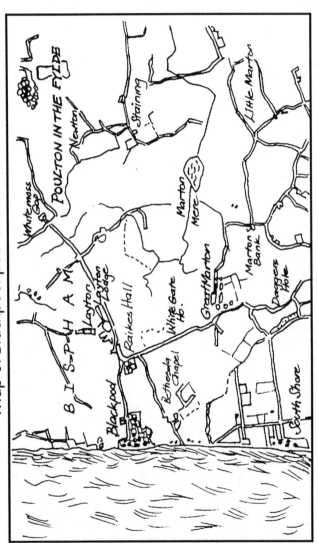

Map of Blackpool published in 1897

✤ Why do you think more people were able to come to Blackpool in 1897?

✤ What else had been built to attract holiday makers?

✤ Who would have lived in the cheaper housing built away from the sea?

✤ Study some old photographs/maps of your nearest seaside town.

Tithe maps

This is a part of a tithe map for the local parish made in 1847.

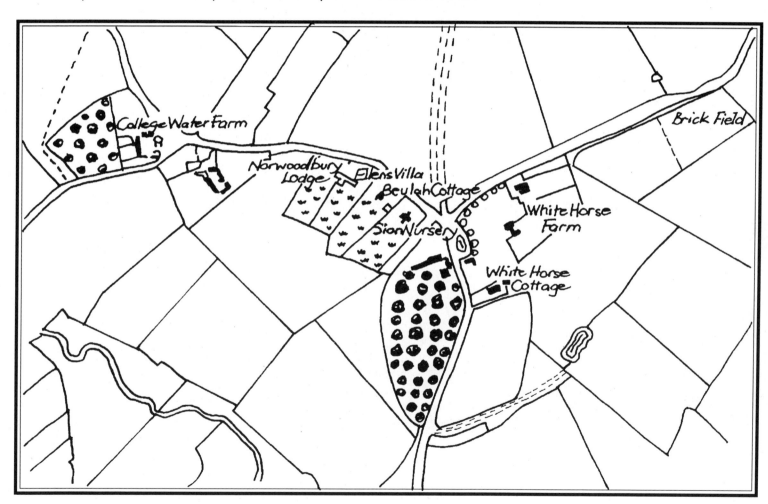

❧ What is a 'tithe'?

❧ Why was it important for the fields to be marked on a tithe map?

❧ What dwelling houses are marked on this map?

❧ How do you think the people living in this area made their living?

❧ Use a tithe map of your area to find out information about the past.

Early settlements

Early settlements

✤ Why do you think the people decided to build a settlement in this place?

✤ Write captions to describe each illustration.

✤ Draw a picture of what the place might look like today.

✤ How has the landscape round your school changed?

Name _____

Farming

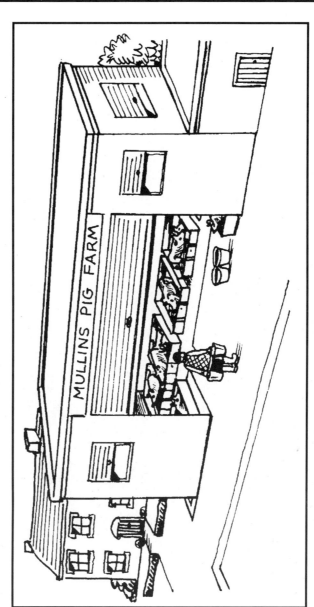

MULLINS PIG FARM

❧ How have changes in pig farming changed the landscape?

❧ This is a pig farm. Write down as many different sorts of farm as you can.

❧ How does a dairy farm change the landscape?

❧ What sort of farm is the nearest to your school?

❧ How has it changed the landscape?

Name _____

A new theme

A new theme

♣ Why do you think the owners of the country house decided to make a theme park?

♣ How do people get to theme parks?

♣ How has the theme park changed the landscape?

Name _____

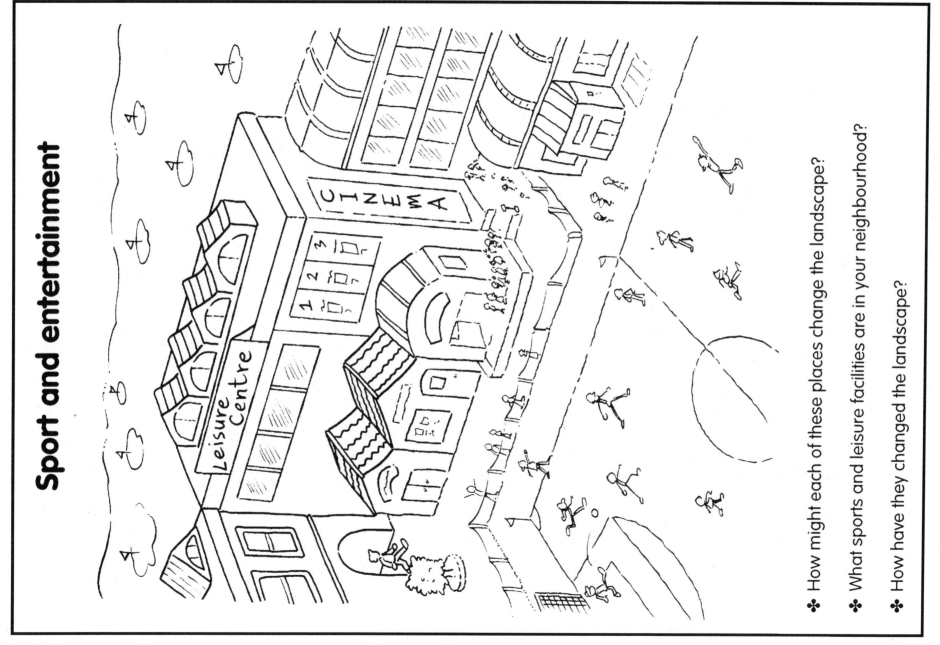

Sport and entertainment

❖ How might each of these places change the landscape?

❖ What sports and leisure facilities are in your neighbourhood?

❖ How have they changed the landscape?

Name _____

Transport

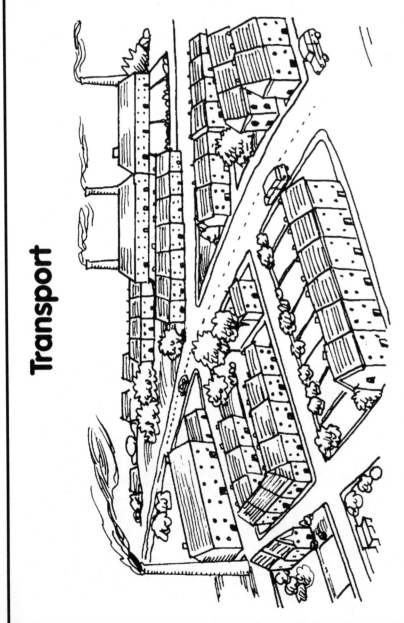

Transport

❖ How have roads changed the landscape in your neighbourhood?

❖ What other forms of transport are there?

❖ How do they change the landscape?

Shopping

❖ How has shopping changed the landscape in each of these three pictures?

♣ What are the advantages of large shopping malls on the outside of towns? What are the disadvantages?

♣ Which is your nearest retail park?

♣ Carry out a survey to see when and where people in your class go shopping. Record the information on a database.

❖ What changes in the landscape have occurred because there have been changes in shopping patterns?

No! No! No!

* What is a village green?

* What do you think is planned for this field?

* How will it change the landscape?

* What messages do the banners give?

* Why do you think the local people feel this way?

* Have there been any protests in your neighbourhood about changes in the landscape?

What's in a name?

Do any of your friends have surnames connected with
occupations in the past such as Butler, Miller, Smith or Farmer?

♣ Write down as many surnames as you can think of like this.

These two drawings show people at work at least 500 years ago.
What surnames might they have been given?

Name _____

Collecting words

✤ Look around your school or neighbourhood. Find and write down some words which:

	I-spy	Where
Give a warning		
Make rules		
Give information to car drivers		
Give information to pedestrians		
An inn sign		
A shop sign		
A sign on the road itself		
Instructions by a machine		
A sign in more than one language		
A road or street sign		
A house name		
An advertisement		

Street names

Many streets are named after special features in the area. Over the years these features may disappear but the road names will stay.

✤ Draw a logo for each of these streets to remind people from where the name comes.

✤ Draw logos for streets and roads near your school.

Mill Street

Bridge Street

Castle View

Market Street

Station Road

Name _____

Guess the street names

Guess the street names

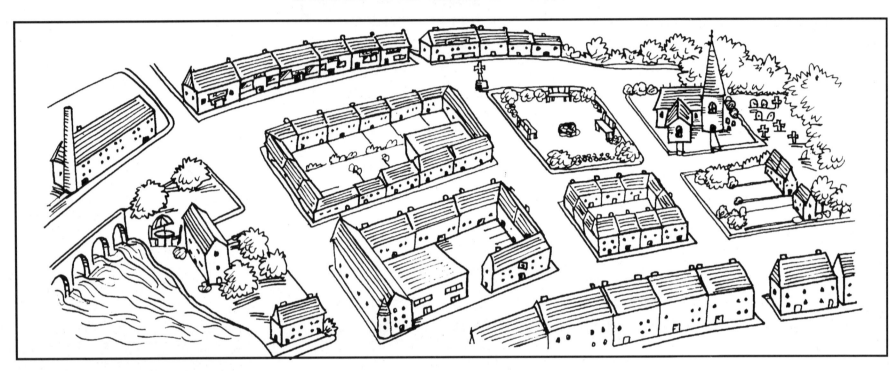

♣ Write these names where you think they go on the map:

Mill Street   Church Street

High Street   Cross Street

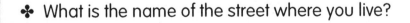

♣ What is the name of the street where you live?

♣ How do you think it got its name?

Travelling names

British place-names can often be found in other countries.

♣ Use a world atlas to find where these UK names travelled to.
Halifax
Boston
Melbourne
Plymouth
South Wales
Newcastle

Why do you think British emigrants named their new homes after places in Britain?

♣ Use the atlas to find some other place-names which have travelled.

♣ Use non-fiction books to find three reasons why people emigrated to these other countries.

Name _____

Celtic place-names

Celtic place-names

Part of name	Meaning
aber	the mouth of a river
ard	height
auchin	a field
bach	small
bal	village
ben	mountain
blair	clearing
caer	fort
cairn	heap of stones
cwn, coombe, coon	valley
cant	corner
craig, carrick, crick	hill
dun	fort
Ffridd	large wood
Inver	mouth of a river
kill	chapel
lin	pool
llan	sacred place
strath	broad valley

❖ The map shows five Celtic place-names. What evidence does each name give about the landscape or buildings near the original settlement?

❖ Use an atlas to put some more Celtic place-names on the map.

❖ What is the nearest place to your school with a Celtic name?

❖ Is there any other evidence of Celtic settlement in your region?

Name _____

Celtic place-names (continued)

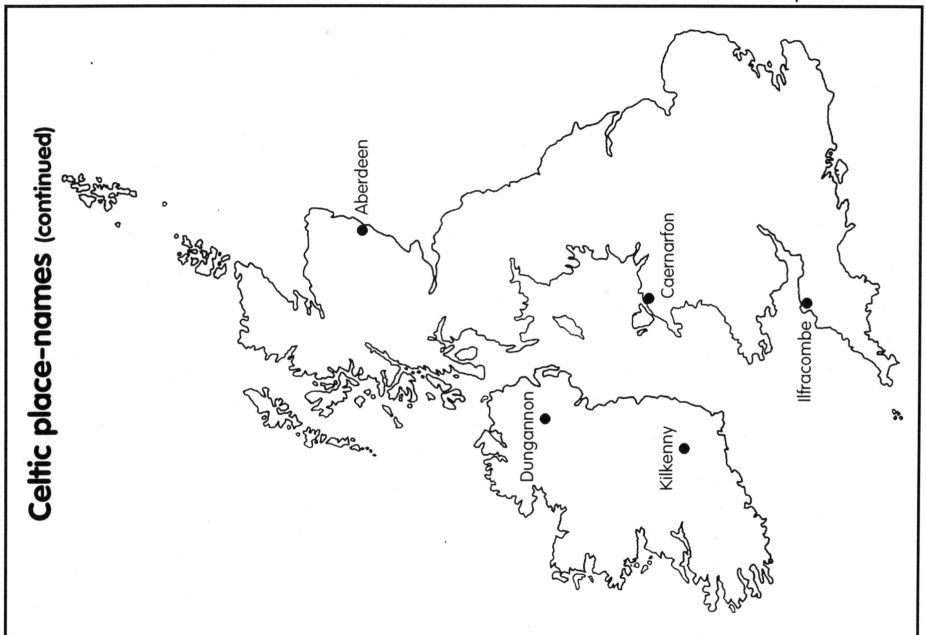

Aberdeen

Caernarfon

Ilfracombe

Dungannon

Kilkenny

A Roman legacy

A Roman legacy

♣ Use a map of Britain to find five towns which have 'caster' or 'chester' in them.
Write them here.

1. _____

2. _____

3. _____

4. _____

5. _____

♣ Use the table below to find out what these words mean.

Part of name	Meaning
caster, cester, chester	fort, camp
port	port
street	road
well	living place

♣ Look at a map of your county or region.
Do the place-names give evidence of Roman settlement?

An Anglo-Saxon legacy

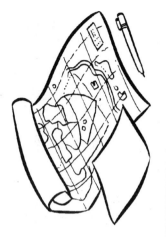

♣ Use a map of your county to find evidence of settlement in Anglo-Saxon times.

♣ Write down any names you can find and use the table to find out how they may have got their name.

Part of name	Meaning
ald	old
beck	brook
bury, brough, borough, burgh	a fortified place
bourne	stream
camb	ridge
chepe	market place
combe	narrow valley
cote, cot, cott	cottage
den, dean, dene	field, valley
don	hill
eld	river crossing
ey	home
ford	place in a forest
ham	wood
hay	the people of
holt, hurst	clearing in a wood

Part of name	Meaning
ing	mound
ley, leigh	lake
low	island
mere, moor	wood
ney, sey	valley
shot	post
slack	place of a building
staple	living place
stead	holy place
stoke	south
stock, stow	village
suther	ford
ton	village
wade	enclosure
wick	settlement
worth	enclosure
wig	heath or shrine

Name _____

Did the Vikings settle near your school?

Did the Vikings settle near your school?

✤ Use a local map and this place-name list to identify any Viking place-names in your area.

✤ Is there any other evidence of Viking settlement in your region?

✤ Use reference books about the Vikings to find out:
• From where they came;
• Some of the reasons why they came.

Part of name	Meaning
austr	east
banke	bank, slope
by	hill, farm
dale, gill, gil	valley
fell	mountain
Fjord	arm of sea between cliffs
foss	waterfall
garth	land, garden
gate	road
Ghyll	mountain track
holm	small island
how	hill, mound
kirk	church
lath	barn
ness, naze	headland
scale	hut
scar	cliff
sea	summer farm
skal	shed
tarn	lake
thorpe, thwaite, toft	village
with	wood

Norman place-names

Part of name	Meaning
beau	beautiful
episcopi	of the Bishop
lieu	place
manor	area owned
mont	hill
vill	village
rouge	red
champ	field

Place-names which have royal or religious names may come from the Normans for example, Abbotsbury and Bere Regis.

♣ Look at a local map for evidence of Norman-French names.

♣ Use reference books or CD-ROMs to find out more about the Normans.
- When did they arrive in England?
- Where did they come from?
- Why did they come?

Movable remains

Name _____

Movable remains

Local museums often contain historical artefacts which have been found nearby. Sometimes very important finds go into National Museums in London, Cardiff, Edinburgh and Belfast.

These objects were found in a drain on the site of the Roman Baths in Bath.

✤ What do you think they are?

✤ How do you think they got into the drain?

✤ Does your local museum have any Roman remains? If so, what kind of items? If not, are there any Celtic remains?

Artefacts in local museums

Name of museum: _____

Date visited: _____

Name of object: _____

Information provided by the museum: _____

_____

_____

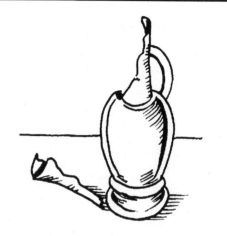

What it looks like now

What it might have looked like

How did it get there?

How did it get there?

✤ Try to write labels for these museum objects.

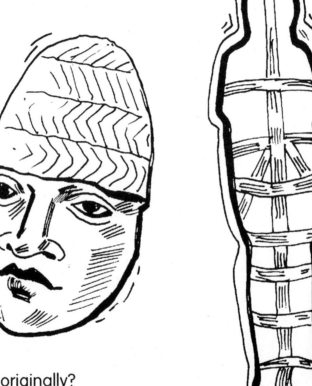

✤ Where do you think they came from originally?

✤ How do you think they got into the museum?

Sometimes local museums have objects which come from different countries.
Find out from your local museum if they have any objects from other countries
and how these objects arrived in the museum.

Name ____________________

Making a class museum (1)

Artefact find sheet

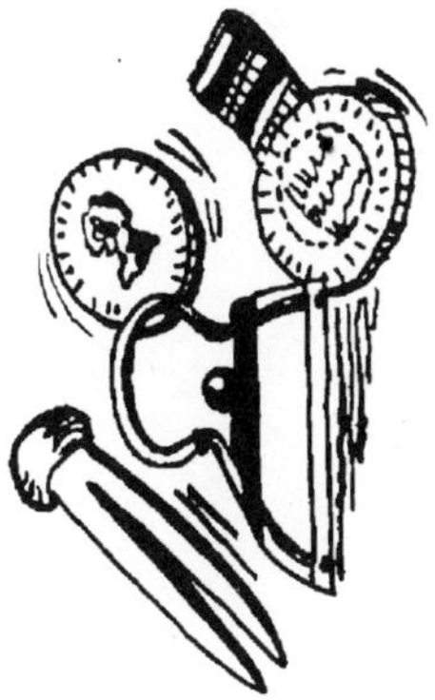

Curator's name: ____________________

Artefact find: ____________________

Description	Observations	Possible uses

Detailed drawing

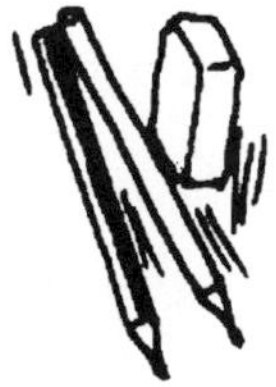

Making a class museum (2)

Artefact fact sheet

Curator's name: _____

Artefact name: _____

Artefact facts

Use

Comments about historical period

Description

Detailed drawing

History at breakfast

Nearly 100 years ago Dr John Kellogg gave his hospital patients cereals made into flakes for their breakfast. His brother William started a company to sell 'corn flakes'.

♣ What is a cereal?

♣ What other cereals have been made into 'flakes' for breakfast?

♣ John and William Kellogg lived in America. Have a look in your cupboards at home and see which other foods originally came from America?

Name _____

Building materials fact sheet

Building materials fact sheet

Materials to identify	✓
Stone	
Cobbles	
Marble	
Chalk	
Clay	
Wood/timber	
Brick	
Tiling	
Iron	
Rendered Walling	
Glass	
Concrete	

knapped flint

gritstone

pointed (embedded in mortar or cement)

uncoursed (irregular blocks)

cobbles

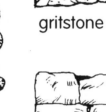

coursed (regular layers)

galleting

Cotswold limestone

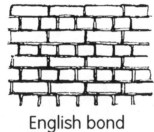

English bond

dry (no cement)

heading bond

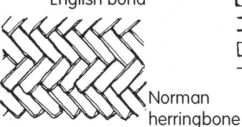

Norman herringbone

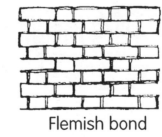

Flemish bond

corner of stones of large ashlar blocks

Roofing fact sheet

Types of Roofing
Thatch
Stone
Slate
Tiles

Source of building materials
locally produced
transported from somewhere else
pre-fabricated buildings

gable

eaves

double pitch

hipped gable

barge boards

single pitch

crow-stepped gable

dutch gable

mansard roof

Doors facts sheet

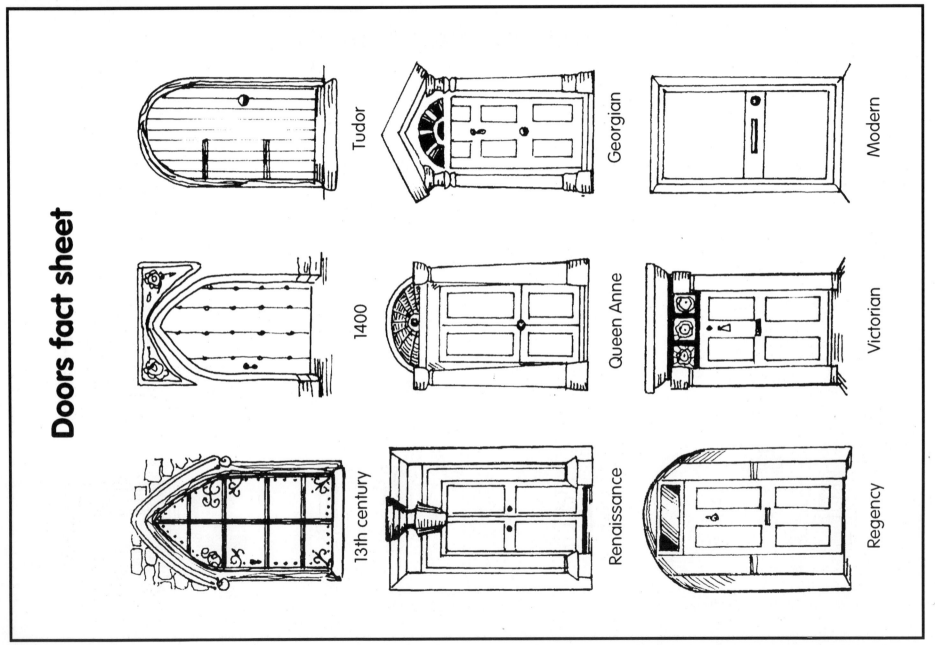

Doors fact sheet

Tudor

Georgian

Modern

1400

Queen Anne

Victorian

13th century

Renaissance

Regency

Windows fact sheet

Early English

1400

Tudor

Wooden Mullion

**Stone frame with
iron bars**

Tudor

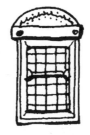

Renaissance

Queen Anne

Georgian

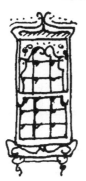

Regency

Victorian

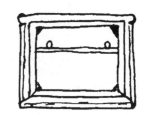

Modern

Local buildings styles fact sheet

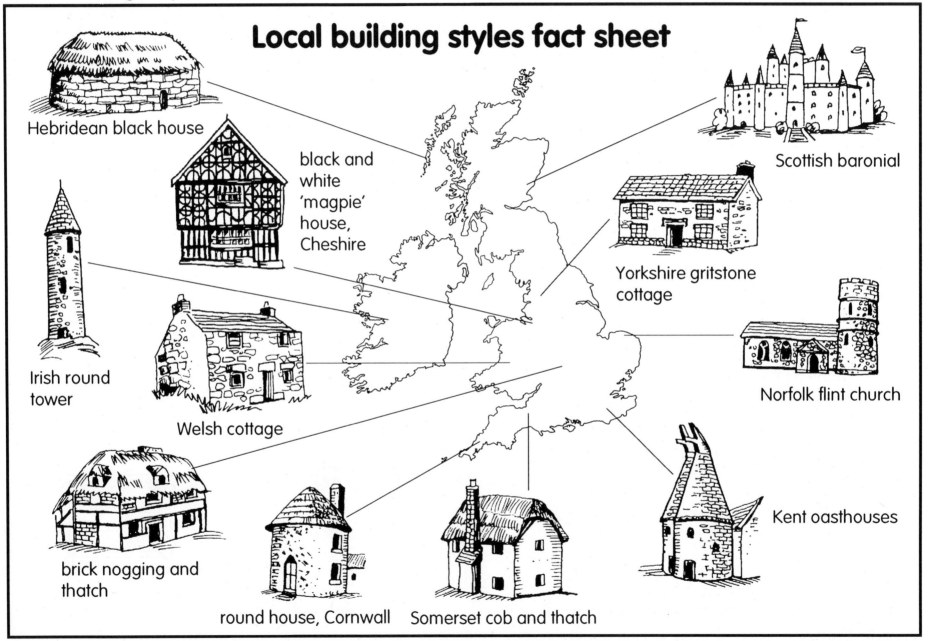

Local building styles fact sheet

Hebridean black house

black and white 'magpie' house, Cheshire

Scottish baronial

Irish round tower

Welsh cottage

Yorkshire gritstone cottage

Norfolk flint church

brick nogging and thatch

round house, Cornwall

Somerset cob and thatch

Kent oasthouses

Reading buildings – questions to ask

Points to look for

✤ What sort of roof does it have?
✤ What materials have been used for the roof?
✤ Are there any decorations on the roof?

✤ Does the house have a chimney? Where is the chimney? What has it been built from? How many chimneys are there?

✤ What materials have been used to build the house?

✤ Have the walls been given an additional layer of material to protect them against the weather?

✤ What shape are the windows?

✤ What kinds of doors does the house have?

✤ Are any doors or windows bricked in?

✤ Is there anything else about the house which makes it unusual?

✤ Is there any evidence of how the house has been changed since it was built?

Name _____

Local architectural features

Local architectural features

✤ Can you put the correct technical names on these features of a house? Use a dictionary to help you. The first one is done for you.

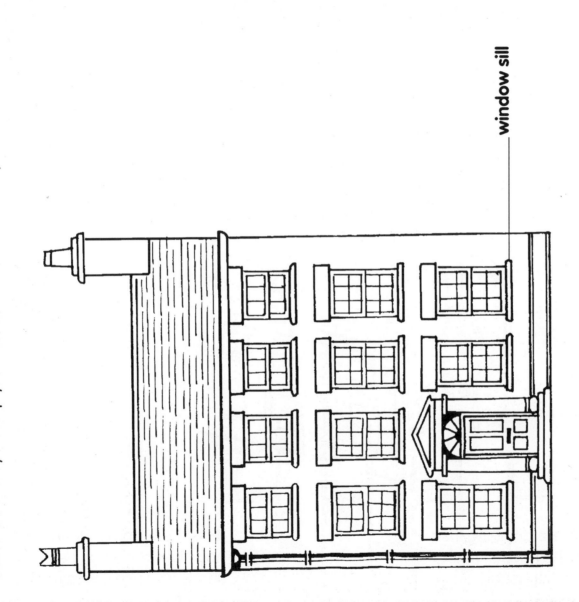

window sill

lintel
pediment
cornice
sash windows
panelled door
fanlight
pillar
plinth

✤ Find a photograph of a local building. On a sheet of paper, draw the building as a diagram like this one. Label as many different parts of the building as you can with the correct words.

Teacher Timesavers: Local history

Historic buildings – ancient Egypt

The Post and Lintel

Some of the earliest builders used the post and lintel principle of construction. Before the invention of the arch they used two vertical beams (posts) to support a horizontal beam (lintel). The Egyptians used papyrus for the posts and the lintel was often a palm log.

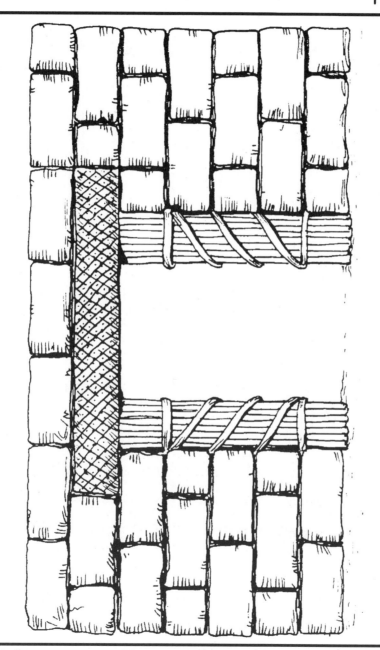

♣ Find examples of the post and lintel method in your neighbourhood.

Further research

♣ Use reference books to find out which group of invaders introduced the rounded arch.

Name _____

Historic buildings – ancient Egypt (continued)

❖ Try this experiment.

You will need:

- two books or wooden blocks;
- several sheets of stiff paper;
- weights.

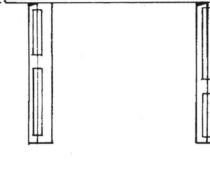

1. one sheet of paper
   Books or wooden blocks

"girders" glued on the sides of accordion-pleated paper

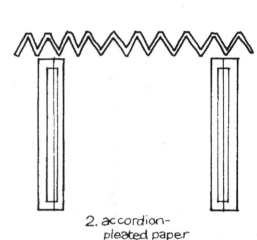

2. accordion-pleated paper

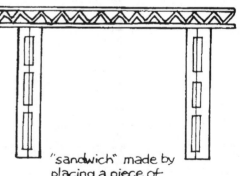

"sandwich" made by placing a piece of paper on the top and one on the bottom of accordion-pleated paper

What to do:
1. Make each of the post-and-lintel designs shown here.
2. Test each construction with weights.
3. Make a table to record your results.

❖ Which design is the strongest?

64

Historic buildings – ancient Greece

Greek columns

Greek architects invented the three 'orders' of architecture. These are called the Doric, Ionic and Corinthian.

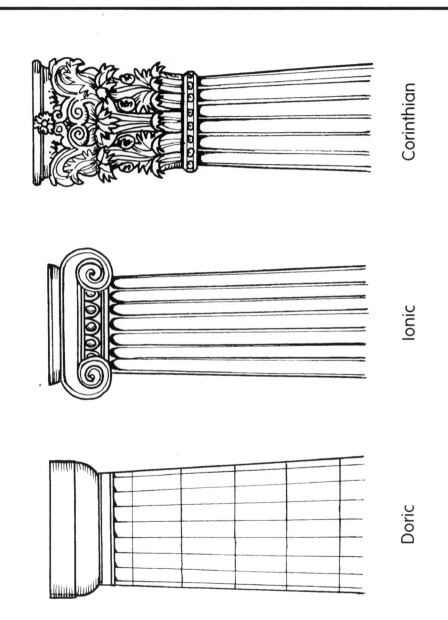

Corinthian

Ionic

Doric

✤ What buildings in your neighbourhood or town have columns? Start a local history architectural journal and draw sketches of these buildings. Try to identify the types of columns in each one.

✤ Use reference books about ancient Egypt and ancient Greece and compare the Egyptian and Greek columns. How do they differ?

Name _____

Historic designs – domes

Historic designs – domes

A dome is like a bowl turned upside down.

❖ Use geostrips to make your own dome.

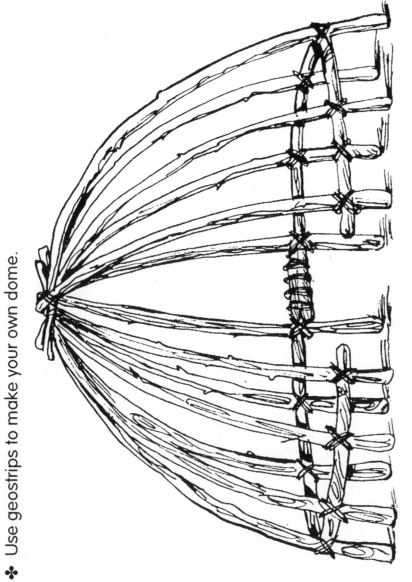

❖ Do any buildings in your locality have domes?
Write down some details about them here.

Name of building	Used for	Year built

Name _____

Why settle here?

✤ These people have decided to build their houses here. Why do you think they have chosen this place?

✤ Use local reference books to find out why people came to live in your area.

✤ Find out why people move into your area today. Do a survey and write your findings here.

Name	Where born	Years lived here	Reasons for moving into the area

✤ Find out why people move away from your area.

The changing story of a settlement

The changing story of a settlement

Tudor

Victorian

Today

Stuart

✤ Cut out these pictures.

✤ Put them in the right order.

✤ Why do you think they go in this order?

✤ Use local resources to make a timeline of your area. Choose three or four stages in its development.

✤ Now draw a picture of what the area round your school might look like in the future.

Village buildings

Old village houses were built with local materials.

✤ Is there any evidence of houses built with these materials near your school?

✤ On the back of this sheet make a plan of the main street of a village near to your school.

✤ Fill in the chart below to show what materials have been used.

Thatch and cob

half-timbering

Wall materials	Roof materials

stone

weather boarding

✤ Did you see any new buildings which have been designed to look like old ones? What features do they have?

Name _____

Village survey

Village survey

Name of village:	Date of visit:	Means of transport:
Historical background	General description of village today	
Buildings observed	Local industry	
Crafts	People interviewed	

Changing cities

Here is an illustration of a large northern town in 1930.

♣ Draw a picture of what you think this view might look like today. Take out buildings you think will have disappeared. Draw what might have taken their place.

Winds and local history

Town Development

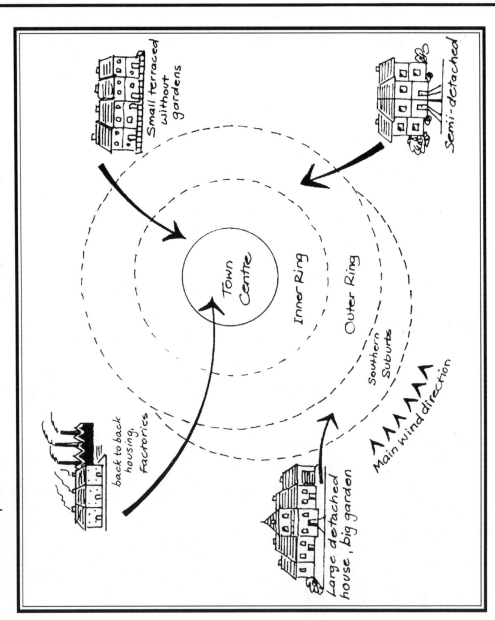

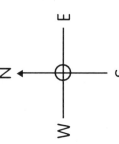

* The diagram shows wind coming from a .... direction.

* Why were the cheapest houses built near the town centre?

* Why were the large detached houses with big gardens built in the southern suburbs?

* Where would factory workers be most likely to live?

* Where would factory owners be most likely to live?

* Where would you most like to live and why?

* How have towns changed from this pattern?

Places of safety and defence

✤ Match the defence to the defenders.

✤ Find out about the nearest hill fort, dyke and castle to your school. Write their names here.

Hill fort	Dyke	Castle

✤ Use reference books to find out more about life in either a hill fort or a castle.

Name _____

Defending the coastline

Defending the coastline

❖ Draw a line to match the illustrations to the defences.

Saxon fort

Martello Tower

Tudor artillery fort

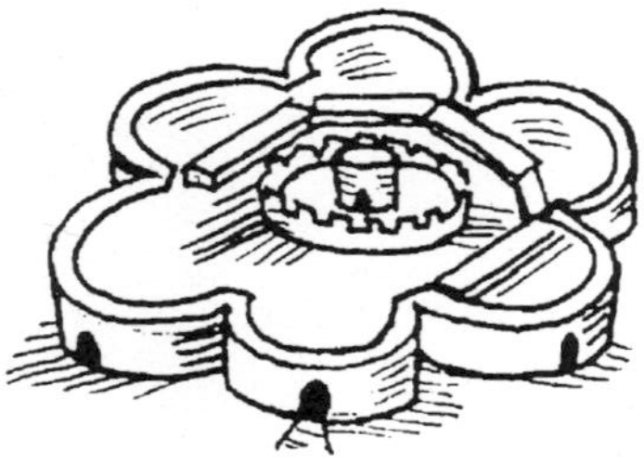

Pill box

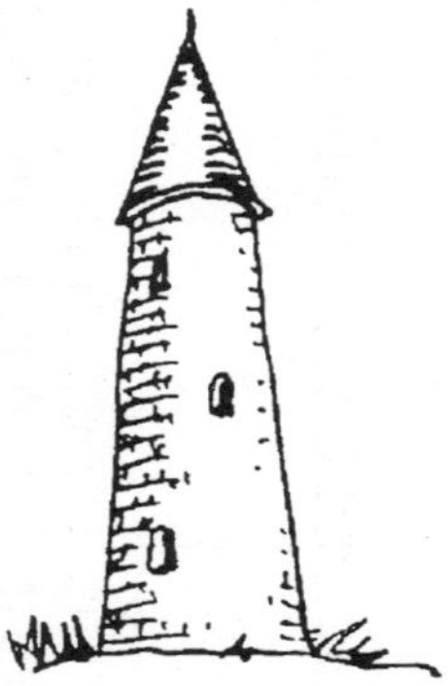

Norman castle

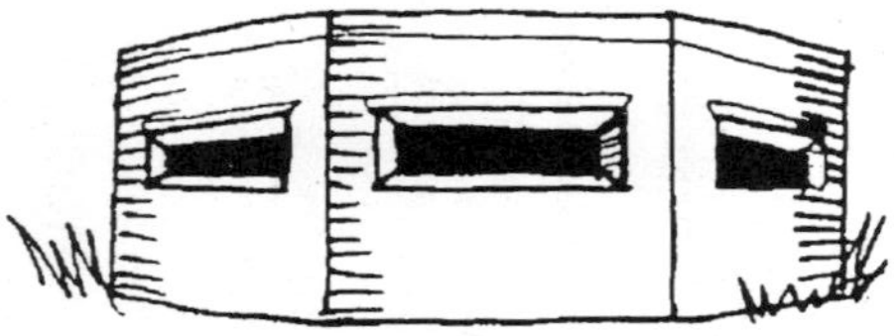

Irish round tower

❖ Cut out the pictures to make a timeline.

❖ How was the coastline nearest to your school defended?

Under attack

✤ If you were the enemy, which way would you come to try to attack this castle?

✤ If you were inside the castle when it was under attack, what would you need?

1. To fight: _____

_____

_____

_____

2. To eat: _____

_____

_____

_____

✤ Put L's where you would place lookouts.

✤ Put G's where you would place guards outside the centre.

✤ What would have to be done to turn your school into a castle?

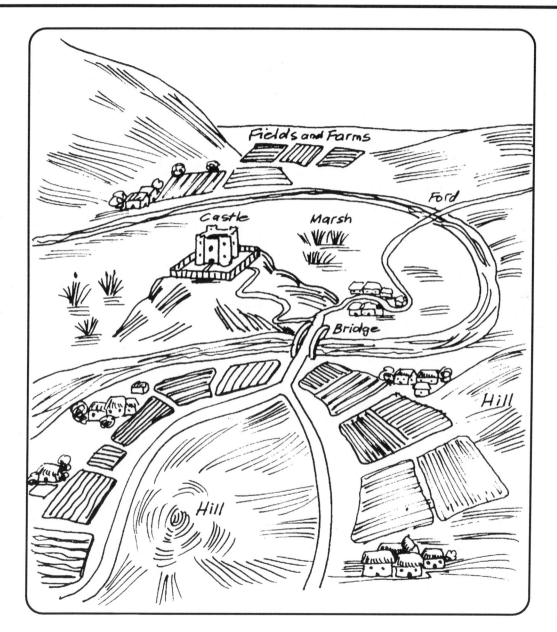

Parts of a castle

✤ Find these things on this map of a castle
and write the numbers where you find them.
Use a reference book to help you.

1	Barbican (outer defence)
2	Moat
3	Gatehouse
4	Corner tower
5	Battlements
6	Motte (mound)
7	Household apartments and the Great Hall
8	Kitchen and pantry
9	Bailey
10	Curtain wall

✤ Draw a diagram of a castle you have visited or have read about.
Why was this site chosen?

✤ Write down the names of any local streets which have the word 'castle' in them.

Spot the difference – houses

1900

142 Victoria Road

Today

142 Victoria Road

✤ Put a circle round some of the things which have changed.

✤ Why do you think these changes have occurred?

✤ Why do you think the road was called Victoria Road?

✤ For homework, look at the outside and inside of your home and see if any changes have been made since it was built.

Inside homes

Name _____

Inside homes

1850

Now

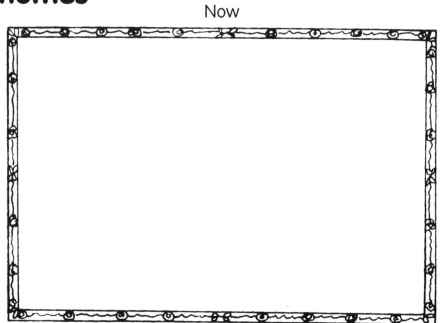

✤ Fill in the table opposite.

✤ Draw your own living room in the space provided above and complete the table.

	1846	Now
Heat		
Light		
Furniture		
Windows		
Doors		

Visiting an old cottage

Sometimes old cottages can be found in open-air museums. This is a plan of an old cottage in Ireland.

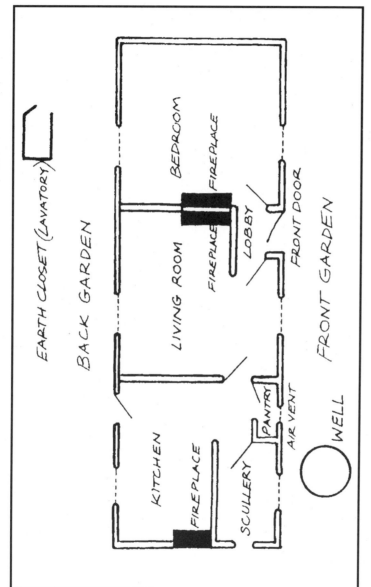

EARTH CLOSET (LAVATORY)

BACK GARDEN

BEDROOM

FIREPLACE

LIVING ROOM

FIREPLACE

LOBBY

FRONT DOOR

FRONT GARDEN

KITCHEN

FIREPLACE

SCULLERY

PANTRY

AIR VENT

WELL

✣ How many rooms are in the cottage?

✣ How many doors and windows can you find?

✣ If you come in the front door which rooms must you go through to reach the kitchen?

✣ Why is there no bathroom in the house?

✣ Where is the toilet?

✣ Where would the water come from for washing?

✣ Draw a plan to show how you would modernise the cottage. You can spend as much money as you want and you can add rooms!

The history of my home

Name _____

The history of my home

Address: _____

_____

Date when it was built: _____

Who has lived in it? _____

_____

_____

What changes have been made to the building?

_____

_____

_____

_____

_____

My home as it is today

My home as it might be in 10 years time

Changing homes

✤ Cut out these pictures and use them to make a housing timeline.

✤ Use a reference book to find out more about the materials used to build one of these homes.

✤ Write an advertisement for the house you have chosen which would encourage someone to buy it.

Visiting a stately home

Name of building: _____

Date visited: _____

1. Plan, sketch or stick a postcard of the front of the building on the back of this sheet.

2. List the main rooms.

3. Choose one room to describe in detail.

4. Use the guide book to find out who has owned and lived in the house since it was built.

5. Who owns it now?

6. Has the house been associated with any famous people and/or events?

7. Does the house have any outbuildings? For what were they used?

8. What are the outbuildings used for now?

Gardens and grounds

Originally, many stately homes which have survived for hundreds of years were virtually self-sufficient. The wealthy owners would have had people farming the land for them.

Nearer to the house there would have been a garden which provided food, flowers and herbs for the household. Herbs would have been used for cooking, medicine and hygiene.

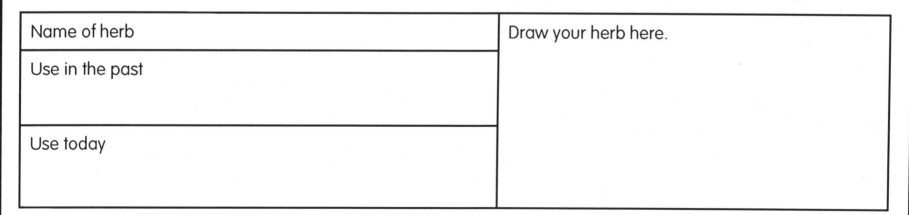

History in herbs

❖ At home, have a look for some herbs. You could look in the garden and in the kitchen. Check the bathroom too.

❖ Choose one herb and research its use today and in the past.

Name of herb	Draw your herb here.
Use in the past	
Use today	

❖ Find out anything else you can about your herb and write it on the back of this sheet.

Name _____

Spot the difference – school

Spot the difference – school

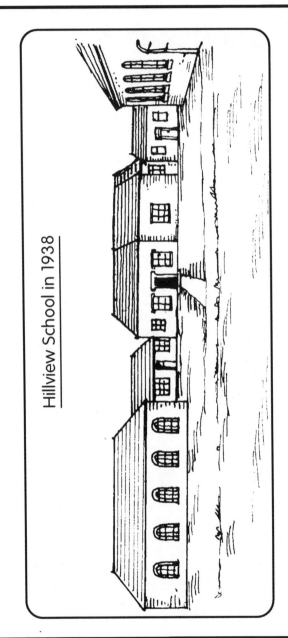

Hillview School in 1938

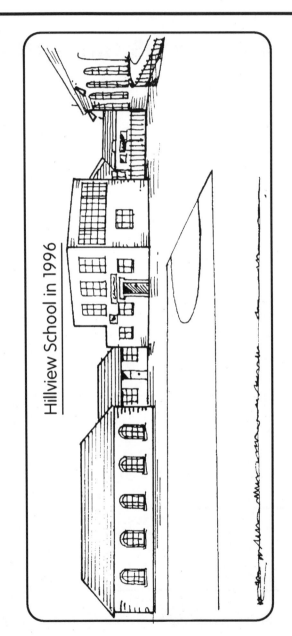

Hillview School in 1996

❖ Put a circle round five things which are the same in both pictures.

❖ Write down or draw five things which are different.

❖ Why do you think the school has changed?

❖ Look at a picture of your school when it was built. How has it changed?

Investigating change in your school

✤ Is your school the first one to be built on this site?

✤ How old is the school?

✤ Has the name been changed?

✤ How many classrooms did it have when it was first built?

✤ How many classrooms does it have today?

✤ Are there any plaques which tell something about the history of the school?

✤ What is the earliest date in the log book?

✤ Other information.

Investigating changes inside your school

Investigating changes inside your school

Name of school: _____

Date built: _____

Is there a foundation stone or plaque? _____

Other memorials:

	Yes	No	If yes, where?
Changes in floor level			
Changes in colour of flooring			
New windows			
New doors			

✤ I think these changes happened because:

Investigating changes outside your school

Name of school: _____

Date built: _____

Is there a foundation stone or plaque? _____

	Yes	No
Any changes in building materials used on external walls?		
Any different coloured bricks?		
Any different coloured cement?		
Blocked windows or doors?		
Differently shaped windows or doors?		
Separate entrances for boys and girls marked?		

❖ I think these have changed because:

Name _____

School log books

The log book is a diary kept by the headteacher to record the important events which take place at a school. This extract comes from a log book.

✤ What national event is recorded on this page of the log book?

✤ What did each child receive as a memento?

✤ If your school was open in 1953, compare the entry in your school log with this one.

✤ Keep a log book for your school for one week.

2.6.53 The Assembly Hall and three classrooms were fitted with television sets. All pupils unable to see the Coronation at home were invited to school. Thus every child on the School Roll, saw Her Majesty, Queen Elizabeth 2 crowned.

3.6.53 Coronation Party held at the school with entertainers provided by the U.D.C and games and competitions organised by Teaching staff.

5.6.53. The Chairman of the Managers presented each pupil with a Coronation Souvenir Pencil

9.6.53 The School Coronation Festival presented to an audience of 530 parents in the open air. The programme included Maypole Dancing, Country Dancing, A Mass P.T Display and a pageant of England through the ages.

16.6.53. The Coronation Festival repeated as a Civic Function.

17.6.53 The Coronation Festival repeated for the Infants.

School log book investigation

Subjects for investigation:

curriculum	buildings	teachers	attendance
holidays	school discipline	children	visitors and inspectors

Punishment book

Punishment book

✤ What years does this page from the book cover?

✤ What type of punishment is recorded here?

✤ What sort of behaviour might end up being punished like this?

✤ What other information does the punishment book give?

✤ Why are children not punished in this way today?

✤ Does your school have an old punishment book? If so, record some of the information it provides.

Date	Punishment given & to whom	By whom	Reason for Punishment
	2 Strokes of the cane		Insolence to
2 - 7 - 52	Harrison P.	F. J Bailey	Mr. Bradford.
	Townsend L.		" "
	Gray P.		" "
	Field S.		" "
	Wright M.		" "
2 - 7 - 52	1 Stroke		
	Misbehaviour repeated		
	J. Kendall		
	Disobedience		
	B. Pertwee		
4. 6. 53	C. Mathews.	F. J. Bailey	repeated disobedience
8. 11. 53	J. Kendall	F. J Bailey	Fireworks in desk.
8. 11. 53	S. Parkes	F. J Bailey	repeated disobedience
8. 11. 53	D. Hunt	F. J Bailey	Late for school. repeatedly

Signs of the trade

❖ Why did shops in the past advertise by picture or sign?

❖ Have a look at some of the local shop signs near your school, and draw some examples.

Inn signs – fact sheet

Old pub/inn signs often record a special local history.

Occupations: The Weavers, The Bakers, The Horseshoe, The Millers, The Wheatsheaf, The Spinning Wheel.

Old Pilgrim Hostels:
The Star, The Seven Stars, The Cross Keys, The Mitre, The Ark, The Bell, The Church House, The Anchor, The Salutation, The Ship, The Lion and Lamb, The Turk's Head (from the Crusades).

Living Creatures:
The Bear, The Lion, The Eagle, The White Hart.

Railway Inns:
The Railway, The Great Western Arms, The Rocket, The Engine, The Railway Arms.

Royal Signs: The Crown, Royal Oaks, The Kings' Arms, The Queens, The Prince of Wales.

Local Connections:
The Derby Arms.

Sports: The Cricketers, The Fisherman, The Fighting Cock.

Old Coaching Names:
The Horse and Groom, The Tollgate, The Chain and Gate, The Turnpike House, Ye Olde Waggon, The Coach and Horses.

Famous People:
The Victoria, The Duke of Wellington, The Nelson Arms, The Catherine Wheel.

River and Canal Names:
The Big Lock, The Tunnel House, The Navigation, The Anchor, The Ship.

Famous Events:
Trafalgar Square, Waterloo, Everest.

Myths and Legends:
The Mermaid, The Dragon, The Unicorn.

Inn signs

Many inn-signs record traditions, people and events from the past.

✤ Use a reference book on inn-signs or a fact sheet to find out what history these four inn signs may record.

✤ Collect the names of inn signs in your area.

✤ Pick one local inn sign and decide what history it records.

✤ Why do you think that newly built pubs often have traditional names?

Bear Hotel

The Queen's Head

The Duke of Wellington

The Fisherman

Name _____

Shopping

Shopping

♣ Look at these two pictures of Littlewoods' stores.

What has changed and what has stayed the same?

Differences	Similarities

♣ Use an information book to find out
what else has changed about shopping.

Now

60 years ago

Local industry map

This is a map of Cheshire in 1801. It shows different industries in the area.

FIRE BRICKS
FLOUR MILLING
PRINTING
BLEACHING
STALYBRIDGE
TEXTILES
PAPER MANUFACTURE
DUKINFIELD
COAL
LONGDENDALE IRON FOUNDRIES
TEXTILES
HYDE
SALT
WALLASEY
CHEMICALS
SOAP
STONE
PORTLINGTON
SALE
STOCKPORT
BREDBURY & ROMILEY
COAL
TEXTILES
BIRKENHEAD
ALTRINGHAM
CHEADLE
MARPLE
COAL
TEXTILES
HOYLAKE
BOWDON
LYMM
FATLEY
HAZELGROVE
WILMSLOW
WIRRAL
FLOUR MILLING
BRAMHALL
FLOUR MILLING
TEXTILES
BEBINGTON
RUNCORN
KNUTSFORD
ALDERLEY
EDGE
BOLLINGTON
CLOTHING
TEXTILES
NESTON
ELLESMERE PORT
Frodsham
MACCLESFIELD
COAL
CHESTER
WINSFORD
NORTHWICH
MIDDLEWICH
CONGLETON
TEXTILES
CHEMICALS
LEAD
ROPE
TEXTILES
TOBACCO
SANDBACH
SALT
CREWE
ALSAGER
IRON FOUNDRY
TEXTILES
NANTWICH
CLOTHING
LEATHER GOODS
SALT

* Make a graph to show the type of industries found in Cheshire in 1801.

* Which industry was the most common?

* What other information does your graph give you?

* Which of these industries would have existed in your area in 1801?

* Try and find out what other industries there were.

Name _____

Factory Site

This is a picture taken from an area in the 1930s. After the picture had been taken labels were put on to the building.

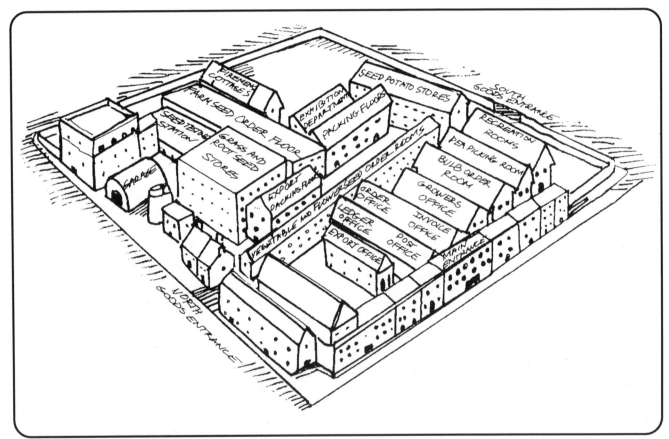

♣ Make a list of the different offices, warehouses and packing buildings.

♣ What do you think the factory was producing?

♣ Why do you think there were firemen's cottages on the site?

♣ What were the main local industries in your area in the 1930s?

♣ What has happened to them since 1930?

Waterways

Until 200 years ago it was quicker and cheaper to send goods to towns by water than to use the roads. Small sailing boats took goods to towns and villages situated alongside rivers. Later canals were built.

Local names and old buildings may provide clues about old river ports:

• place names like port, hythe, quay, wharf;

• road names like Eastgate Wharf, River Wharf, Customs House Street;

• inn names like The Ship, The Crown and Anchor;

• buildings such as old warehouses, factories near rivers, mills or quays.

❖ Which is the nearest old river port to your school?

❖ Which is the nearest canal to your school?

❖ Use a map of your nearest town and look at the clues above to find out if it was once a port.

Railways

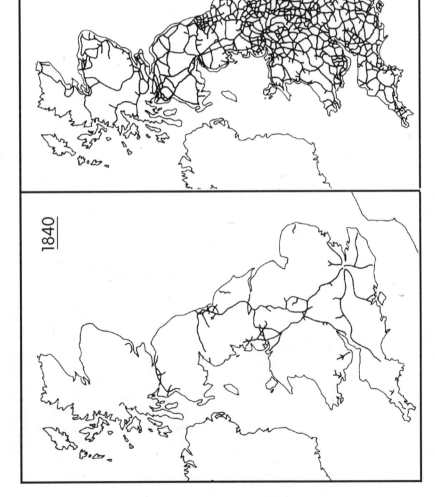

1900

1840

Railways

* What story do the two maps show?

* Which is the nearest station to your school?

* What historical evidence is there in your area of a former railway line?

* Use local reference books to find out about the history of the railway in your area.

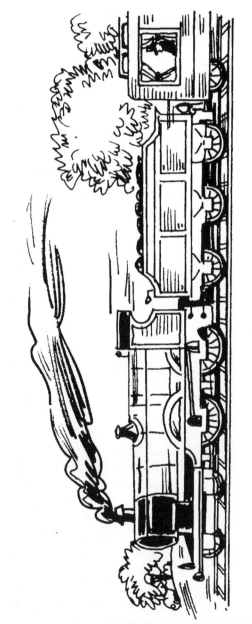

I-spy historic roads

What to look for	What it may mean	Name of road/ street or area
Two or three place-names in the same district such as causeway, stone, stratford, stret, ridgeway.	A Roman Road nearby.	
A straight country road making right angle turns for no reason.	A Roman Road following boundaries of Roman fields.	
Toll house – cottage built near a major road junction or near an old bridge.	Road built in the 18th century. Money collected from travellers by the gatekeeper in the toll house.	
Names such as 'The Old Toll House' or part of a town or village with 'toll' in its name.	18th century toll road.	
Narrow bridge over water with a low wall.	Medieval road.	
Old pub with religious name.	Resting place for medieval travellers originally run by a religious order.	
Milestones.	18th century road. Milestones had to be built at regular intervals.	
A pub which might have started as a coaching inn – stables at the back.	Old coach road and the pub would be used by the wealthy travelling by stage coach.	

✣ Play 'I Spy' when you are travelling. Look for some of these clues, write down the name of the street where you saw them.

✣ Collect images of places in you local area which show these features and which tell you about the history of local roads.

✣ Use reference books to find out more about the history of roads.

Streets

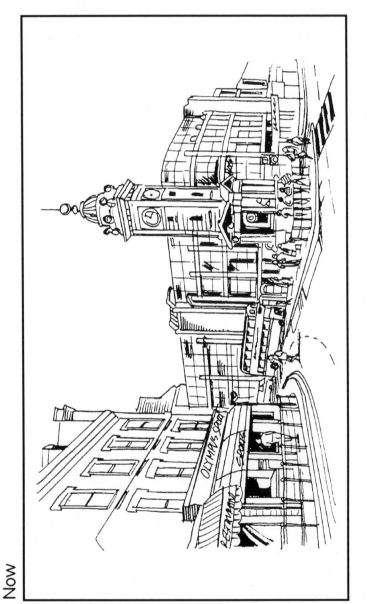

Now

Then (1900)

♣ Compare these pictures. Circle some of the things which have changed. Why have they changed?

♣ On a piece of paper, draw a picture of the same street in 100 years time. Do you think anything will still be the same?

Street furniture

fountain

Where? _____

railings

Where? _____

bollard

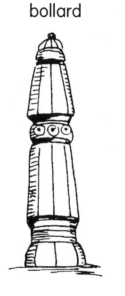

Where? _____

_____

cobblestones

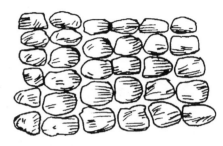

Where? _____

footscraper

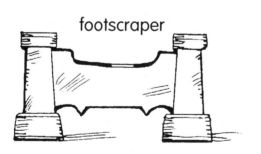

Where? _____

spur stone

Where? _____

✤ Can you find any examples of street furniture like this in your area?
✤ Why did people need foot scrapers?

Name _____

Royal Mail

❖ Look at these post boxes. Can you tell which monarch's initials are shown on them?

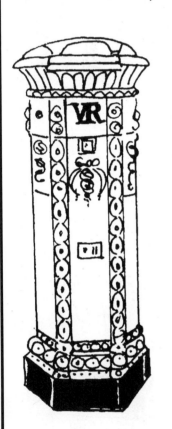 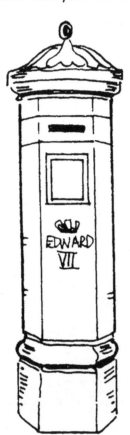 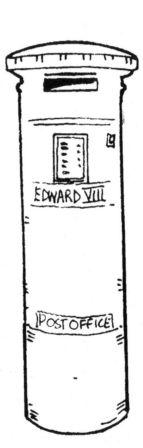  

❖ Record the initials in chronological order.

❖ Draw the oldest post-box in your neighbourhood.

❖ How many different-shaped boxes can you find?

❖ Why is the monogram (initials) for Edward VIII very rare?

I-spy street lights

✤ Are there any street lights like these near your school?

  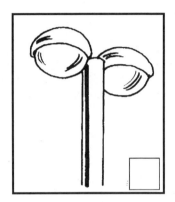 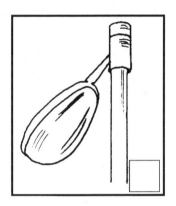 

✤ Put a tick next to any of them you have seen near your school or home.

✤ Choose a street light you have seen near your school and draw it.

✤ Use a reference book about streets to find out when streets were first lit by electricity.

Name _____

Street entertainment

❖ Use a reference book about streets to find pictures or photographs of different forms of street entertainment in the past and make a list of them below.

Street Entertainment	Period
Barrel organ	Victorian

❖ What street entertainments are there today in your nearest town?

Skeleton of a community

Buildings

❖ Cut out these pictures and arrange them in chronological order.

❖ Your nearest town may have buildings like these. Check whether it does and collect postcards, photographs and illustrations of them.

❖ Does your town have any other important buildings, such as a theatre, a castle or a football stadium? Find out when they were built. The local Tourist Information bureau may have information about the town.

❖ Use all your pictures to make a local buildings timeline. Do you notice anything about when the buildings were built?

Recording evidence of change

Name of building: _____

Date visited: _____

♣ Find four things on the outside of a local
building which have been added since it was built.

1. _____

2. _____

3. _____

4. _____

♣ Find four things that tell you the building is old.

1. _____

2. _____

3. _____

4. _____

♣ Find four places where the building has been repaired.

1. _____

2. _____

3. _____

4. _____

A new lease of life

Here are four buildings which have changed in their use.

♣ What do you think they were in the past?

1. The nursing home was _____

2. The house was _____

3. The carpet warehouse was _____

4. The restaurant was _____

♣ Here is an old school up for sale. For what could it be used?

♣ Find some buildings in your area which have been given a new lease of life. Write down what they were used for originally, what they are used for now and draw them.

Plaques on buildings

Plaques on buildings

GLADSTONE
FOUR TIMES
PRIME MINISTER
BORN
IN THIS HOUSE
29TH DECEMBER 1809

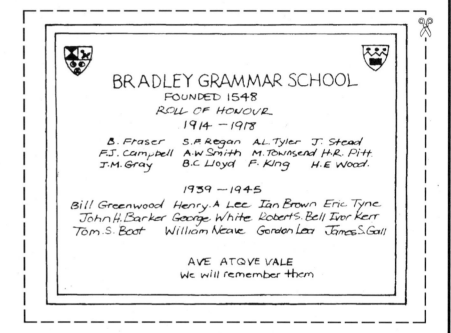

BRADLEY GRAMMAR SCHOOL
FOUNDED 1548
ROLL OF HONOUR
1914 – 1918

B. Fraser   S.F. Regan   A.L. Tyler   J. Stead
F.J. Campbell A.W Smith   M. Townsend   H.R. Pitt.
J.M. Gray   B.C Lloyd   F. King   H.E Wood.

1939 – 1945

Bill Greenwood   Henry.A Lee   Ian Brown   Eric Tyne
John H. Barker   George White   Robert S. Bell Ivor Kerr
Tom.S. Boot   William Neave   Gordon Lea   James S.Gall

AVE ATQVE VALE
We will remember them

Plaques like these are erected to record information about people and events from the past. Sometimes a plaque just records the date the building was completed. Foundation plaques record when buildings were started.

❖ Cut these plaques out and put them in chronological order.

❖ Can you find a plaque in or near your school? Copy down what the plaque says and draw it.

❖ Can you find a plaque for an animal? Copy it and draw it too.

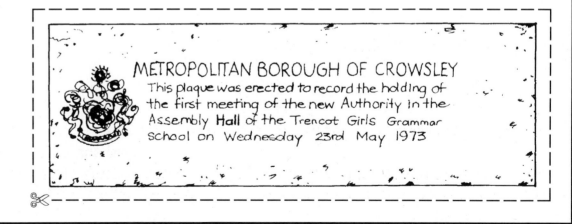

METROPOLITAN BOROUGH OF CROWSLEY
This plaque was erected to record the holding of the first meeting of the new Authority in the Assembly **Hall** of the Trencot Girls Grammar School on Wednesday 23rd May 1973

Memorials

Sometimes memorials are put up long after an event has happened. This is an illustration of some memorial tiles which can be found in an underground passage in the city of Plymouth. The tiles mark some famous people and events in history.

♣ Were all these people remembered for good reasons?

MARY 1553-58

ELIZABETH I 1558 - 1603
RESTORED THE PROTESTANT RELIGION
SUPPORTED THE ENGLISH SEA DOGS
KNIGHTED SIR FRANCIS DRAKE ABOARD THE GOLDEN HIND AT DEPTFORD

SIR THOMAS CAVENDISH NAVIGATOR THE SECOND ENGLISHMAN TO SAIL ROUND THE WORLD

SIR JOHN HAWKINS 1532 - 1595 A PLYMOUTH MAN CONTROLLER OF THE QUEEN'S SHIPS HE STARTED THE SLAVE TRADE AS A REAR ADMIRAL HE COMMANDED THE VICTORY AT THE DEFEAT OF THE SPANISH ARMADA.

1553 RESTORATION OF THE ROMAN CATHOLIC RELIGION 1587 EXECUTION OF MARY QUEEN OF SCOTS

♣ Use a reference book to find out more about the events recorded.

♣ What other important events happened between 1558 and 1603?

♣ Can you find anything in your community which may have existed in the Tudor period?

♣ Can you find out about a gift which has been given to your community in memory of an important event or to record the life of an important person?

Monuments in time

Monuments in time

Celtic Cross

Nelson's Column

Hadrian's Wall

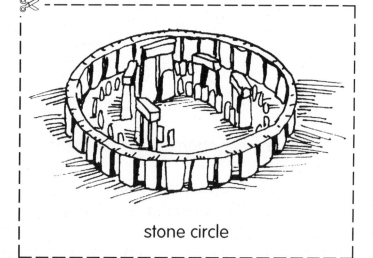

stone circle

♣ Cut out and arrange these monuments in chronologial order.

♣ Use a reference book on monuments to find out more about the purpose of each of these monuments.

♣ Find a monument near your school and draw it. Why was it built? When was it put in?

A place to worship

All these places are used for worship.
❖ Tick any that you have seen like this in your neighbourhood.

❖ How many different kinds of religious buildings can you see near you?

❖ Find out the dates when these buildings were first used for worship.

War memorials

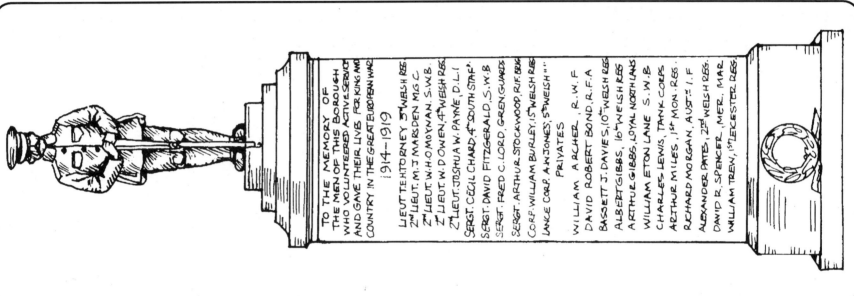

TO THE MEMORY OF
THE MEN OF THIS BOROUGH
WHO VOLUNTEERED ACTIVE SERVICE
AND GAVE THEIR LIVES FOR KING AND
COUNTRY IN THE GREAT EUROPEAN WAR
1914-1919

LIEUT T.E.H.TORNEY 5TH WELSH REG.
2ND LIEUT. M.J MARSDEN M.G.C.
2ND LIEUT. W.H.O MOYNAN. S.W.B.
2ND LIEUT. W.D OWEN, 4TH WELSH REG
2ND LIEUT. JOSHUA W. PAYNE, D.L.I
SERGT. CECIL CHARD, 4TH SOUTH STAFF.
SERGT. DAVID FITZGERALD, S.W.B
SERGT. FRED C. LORD, GREN. GUARDS
SERGT. ARTHUR STOCKWOOD, RIF. BRIG.
CORP. WILLIAM BURLEY, 1ST WELSH REG.
LANCE CORP. A.N JONES, 5TH WELSH "...."
PRIVATES

WILLIAM ARCHER, R.W.F
DAVID ROBERT BOND, R.F.A
BASSETT J. DAVIES, 10TH WELSH REG.
ALBERT GIBBS, 16TH WELSH REG.
ARTHUR GIBBS, LOYAL NORTH LANS.
WILLIAM ETON LANE S.W.B
CHARLES LEWIS, TANK CORPS
ARTHUR MILES, 1ST MON. REG.
RICHARD MORGAN, AUST.L I.F
ALEXANDER PATES, 2ND WELSH REG.
DAVID R. SPENCER, MER. MAR.
WILLIAM TREW, 1ST LEICESTER REG.

War memorials

All over the world there are famous war memorials and museums which record the sufferings of people.

♣ Which war does this war memorial at Cowbridge, South Glamorgan commemorate?

♣ Do any of the same family names appear?

♣ What regiments or branches of the armed forces are recorded?

♣ Visit the nearest war memorial to your school and record some of the information on it.

♣ Find out the names of any two internationally-known war memorials and write them down.

A Sikh gurdwara

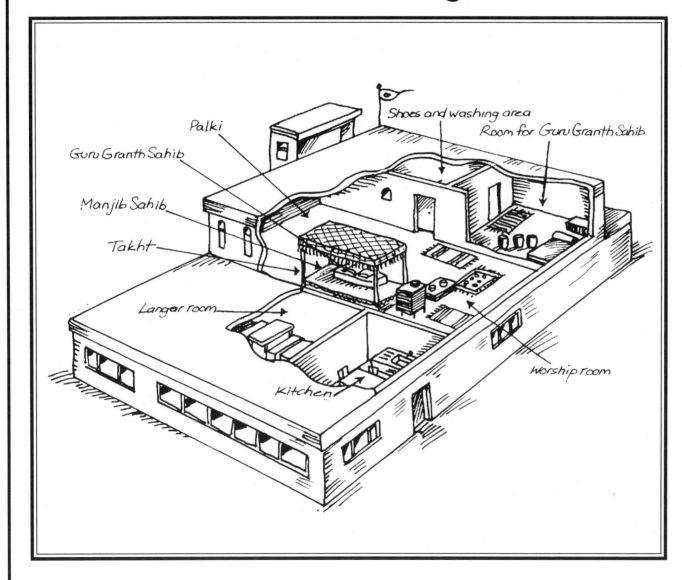

Palki

Shoes and washing area

Room for Guru Granth Sahib

Guru Granth Sahib

Manjib Sahib

Takht

Langar room

Kitchen

Worship room

✤ Use reference books about the Sikh faith to find out more about the history behind the gurdwara.

✤ Find out where the most famous gurdwara is?

✤ Where is the nearest gurdwara to your school?

Name _____

A mosque

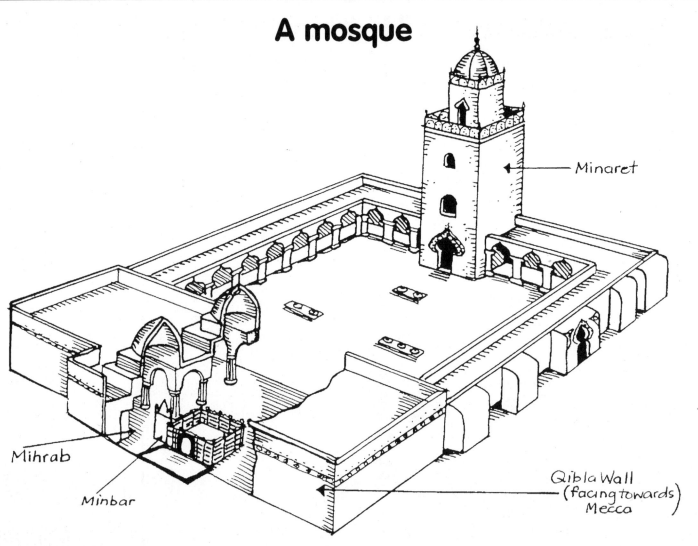

A mosque

Minaret

Mihrab

Minbar

Qibla Wall
(facing towards)
Mecca

❖ Find out more about the nearest mosque to your school.
When was it built?
Has it always been a mosque?

Changing churches

❖ Record what was built and when.

11th Century	Nave, Chancel
13th Century	
15th Century	
19th Century	

♣ What is happening to many churches today?

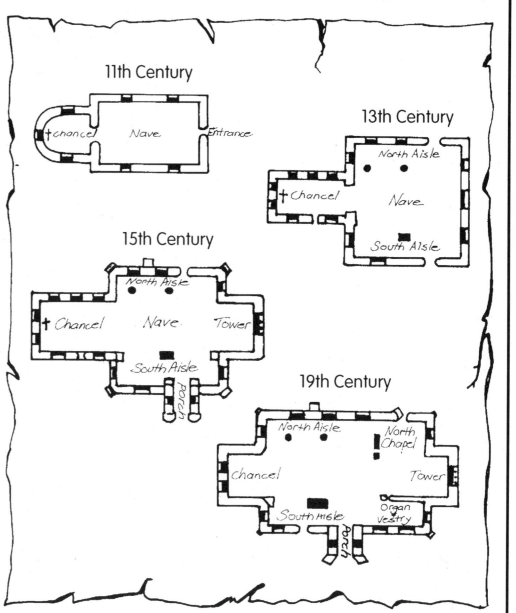

11th Century

chancel   Nave   Entrance

13th Century

North Aisle

Chancel   Nave

South Aisle

15th Century

North Aisle

Chancel   Nave   Tower

South Aisle   Porch

19th Century

North Aisle   North Chapel

Chancel   Tower

South Aisle   Organ Vestry   Porch

Church check list

Church check list

✤ Draw a plan of the outside of your local church.

✤ Does your church have these features? Put a tick or a cross for each one:

	Feature	Yes	No
	a tower		
	a spire		
	a clock		
	a sundial		
	gargoyles		
	a lychgate		
	a parapet		
	a weather vane		

✤ What makes your church special to the people who worship there?

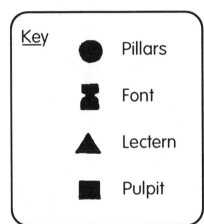

Village church

✤ Look at this plan of the inside of a village church.

Key

●   Pillars

⬗   Font

▲   Lectern

■   Pulpit

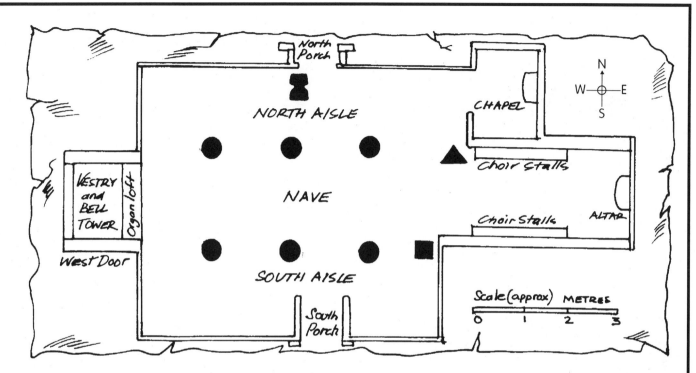

✤ Write down your answers to these questions.

1. At which end is the altar? _____

2. How many porches are there? _____

3. What separates the side aisles from the nave? _____

4. How long is the church? _____

5. What is the area of the church in m²? _____

Church furniture

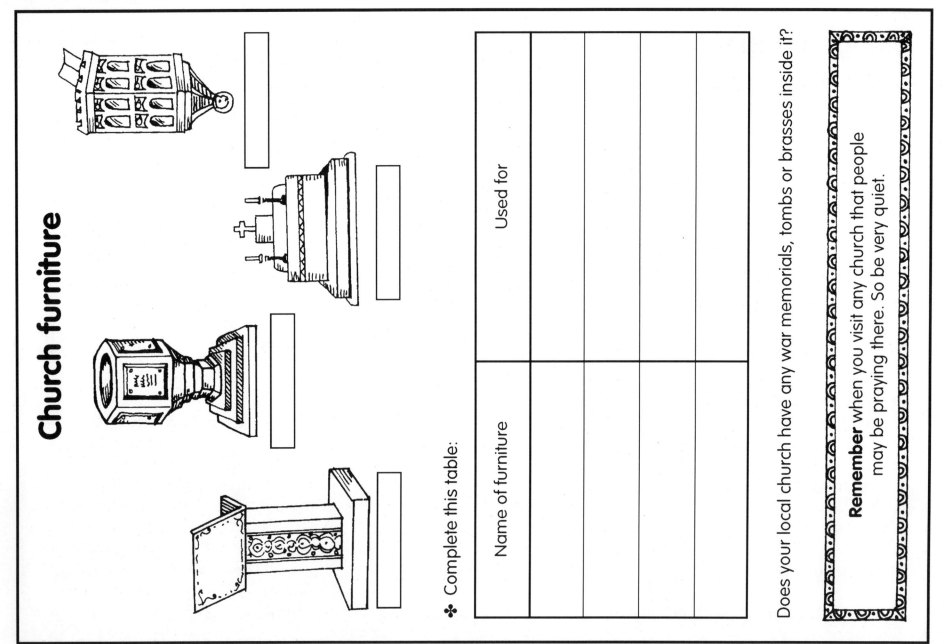

Church furniture

❖ Complete this table:

Name of furniture	Used for			

Does your local church have any war memorials, tombs or brasses inside it?

Remember when you visit any church that people may be praying there. So be very quiet.

Chapels

Some villages have chapels.

♣ Is there a chapel near you? Draw a picture of it on a separate piece of paper.

♣ Make a plan of the inside of the chapel, and label the most important parts.

Does your nearest chapel look like the one in the picture here? Write down the things which are the same and the things which are different.

Differences	Similarities

♣ To which religious group does your chapel belong?

Are there any other buildings connected with it such as a Sunday School building, a minister's house, manse or a church school?

♣ Find out about the history of your chapel and write a short piece about it. Say when it was built and record any important events or people connected with it.

Using plans

Using plans

This is a plan of Fountains Abbey in Yorkshire. It was built in 1132 and destroyed by Henry VIII when the monasteries were dissolved. The plan is made up from evidence provided by the ruins.

❖ Try to find out why the monastery was destroyed.

❖ Why do people visit ruins?

❖ Use a book about monasteries to find the meanings for these words.

Word	Meaning
infirmary	
abbot	
cloister	
refectory	
lay brothers	
chapter house	
cellarium	

❖ Which of these words have you heard used today?

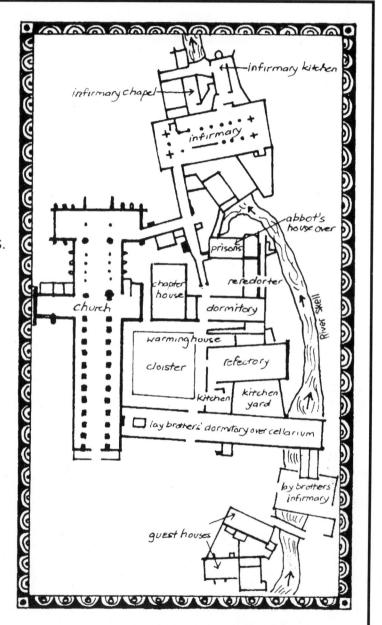

Roman numerals – fact sheet

I – 1	XI – 11	XXX – 30
II – 2	XII – 12	XL – 40
III – 3	XIII – 13	L – 50
IV – 4	XIV – 14	C – 100
V – 5	XV – 15	CC – 200
VI – 6	XVI – 16	CCC – 300
VII – 7	XVII – 17	CD – 400
VIII – 8	XVIII – 18	D – 500
IX – 9	XIX – 19	CM – 900
X – 10	XX – 20	M – 1000

John Samuel Taylor
Born December x
MDCCXLV

Died February 6ᵗʰ
in the year of our Lord
1792

<u>Test yourself:</u>

If LXVI is 66, how would
you write 97?

 Look at this gravestone.
What year was this man
born in?

_____

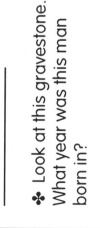 Write in Roman numerals
what year he died.

_____

Graveyards – fact sheet

Graveyards – fact sheet

❖ Write and draw what you found out about:

Plant and animal life.	Different types of lettering.

Materials used to build gravestones.

Symbols used for death		✓
hour-glass		
bones		
wings		
angels		
weeping willow		
skulls		
skeletons		

❖ Tick here if you saw any children's tombstones.

❖ Fill out the table below to show the changes in mortality rates by writing in the ages of ten men and women when they died, over periods of 50 years.

1850 – 1900		
1800 – 1850		
1900 – 1950		

122

Teacher Timesavers: Local history

Unusual epitaphs

❖ Do you know what an epitaph is?

❖ Write down which of these epitaphs would not be found in a church. How do you know this?

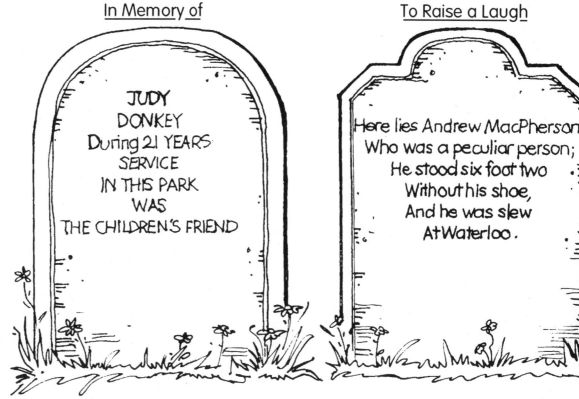

For the Famous

Shakespeare
Good friend, for Jesu's
sake forbeare
To digg the dust
enclosed heare;
Blessed be ye man yt
spares these stones,
And curst be he yt
moves my bones.

In Memory of

JUDY
DONKEY
During 21 YEARS
SERVICE
IN THIS PARK
WAS
THE CHILDREN'S FRIEND

To Raise a Laugh

Here lies Andrew MacPherson
Who was a peculiar person;
He stood six foot two
Without his shoe,
And he was slew
At Waterloo.

❖ Are there any unusual tombs, crosses or memorials in your local churchyard? Do any tombs have railings around them? Why do you think they are there?

❖ Do any of the tombstones record a local disaster, accident or outbreak of disease?

Reading gravestones

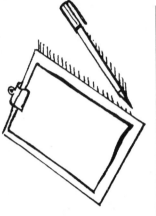

Reading gravestones

♣ What historical evidence does this old family gravestone provide about the Sedgwick family?

Complete this chart:

Family Name	First Name	Born	Died

♣ Did you find out anything else?

Richard. H. Smith
Son of Terry and May Smith
who died 6th September 1811
aged 3 months

Carol their daughter
died 21st November 1813
aged 20 months

Carol another daughter
died 5th September 1819
aged 12 months

John their son
died January 19th 1827
aged 17 years and 2 months

May, wife of Terry Smith
died November 7th 1828
aged 49 years and 9 months

Terry Smith
died 26th June 1829
aged 49 years and 7 months

The census

♣ This is part of a census form for one family.

No of Schedule	ROAD, STREET, & Co. and No. or NAME of HOUSE	NAME and Surname of each Person	RELATION to Head of Family	CONDITION as to Marriage	AGE Last Birthday		Rank, Profession or OCCUPATION	WHERE BORN
					Males	Females		
285	27 Moses St.,	Henry Wilkins	Head	Mar	45		Pensioner from Royal Navy	Falmouth, Cornwall
		Jessie Wilkins	Wife	Mar		32		Scotland
		Mabel Wilkins	Dau			6	Scholar	Liverpool, Lancashire
		Ethel Wilkins	Dau			3	Scholar	Liverpool, Lancashire

The undermentioned Houses are Situate within the Boundaries of the — Page

Civil Parish (or Township) of — City or Municipal Borough of — Municipal Ward of — Parliamentary Borough of — Town or Village or Hamlet of

♣ What does it tell you?

♣ Who lives at 27 Moses Street?

♣ How many children are in the family?

♣ Draw a picture of this family and write the first names under each person.

♣ Now try making a census form for your family.

Census research 1

Name _____

The undermentioned Houses are Situate within the Boundaries of the				Page		
Civil Parish (or Township) of	City or Municipal Borough of		Municipal Ward of	Parliamentary Borough of		Town or Village or Hamlet of

No of Schedule	ROAD, STREET, & Co. and No. or NAME of HOUSE	NAME and Surname of each Person	RELATION to Head of Family	CONDITION as to Marriage	AGE Last Birthday		Rank, Profession or OCCUPATION	WHERE BORN
					Males	Females		
284	25 Moses St.,	Henry Cowan	Head	Mar	36		Seaman	Bermuda,
		Louisa Cowan	Wife	Mar		29		Bristol, Gloucestershire
		Katherine Cowan	Dau			10		Bristol, Gloucestershire
		Henry Cowan	Son		8			Bristol, Gloucestershire
		Florence Cowan	Dau			6		Bristol, Gloucestershire
		George Cowan	Son		5			Bristol, Gloucestershire
		Marie Cowan	Dau			3		Liverpool, Lancashire
		Edith Cowan	Dau			1		Liverpool, Lancashire
		Child unchristened	Dau			1 mth		Liverpool, Lancashire
		Caroline Jackson	Mother in law	Mar		56		Redball, Devonshire
		George Cowan	Brother	Unmar	33		Seaman	Bermuda
285	27 Moses St.,	Henry Wilkins	Head	Mar	45		Pensioner from Royal Navy	Falmouth, Cornwall
		Jessie Wilkins	Wife	Mar		32		Scotland
		Mabel Wilkins	Dau			6	Scholar	Liverpool, Lancashire
		Ethel Wilkins	Dau			3	Scholar	Liverpool, Lancashire
286	28 Moses St.,	Margaret Buttery	Head	Wid		32		Liverpool, Lancashire
		Elizabeth Buttery	Dau	Unmar		18		Liverpool, Lancashire
		Charles Buttery	Son		10 mths			Liverpool, Lancashire
287	31 Moses St.,	Jonathan Chapman	Head	Mar	53		Greengrocer	Patterdale, Westmorland
		Mary Chapman	Wife	Mar		50		Greystoke, Cumberland
		Elizabeth Chapman	Dau	Unmar		15		Carslisle, Cumberland
		Jonathan Chapman	Son	Mar	23		Schoolmaster	Greystoke, Cumberland
		Weshullemeth Chapman	Dau in law	Mar		27	Formerly school mistress	Bagley, Yorkshire
288	33 Moses St.,	John Williamson	Head	Mar	49		Collector of Market Tolls	Culgarth, Cumberland
		John Williamson	Son	Unmar	19		Railway servant	Liverpool, Lancashire
		Sarah Williamson	Dau	Unmar		16		Liverpool, Lancashire
		Thomas Williamson	Son		12		Scholar	Liverpool, Lancashire
		Richard Williamson	Son		10		Scholar	Liverpool, Lancashire
		Elizabeth Williamson	Dau			8	Scholar	Liverpool, Lancashire
		Total of males and females						

Teacher Timesavers: Local history

Census research

Look at the census return on the other sheet and answer these questions about your findings:

Number of houses _____

Number of people _____

Number of men _____

Number of women _____

Number of children _____
(18 and under)

Number and age of people born in Liverpool _____

Number of people born outside the city _____

Different occupations _____

_____

_____

❖ What evidence does this provide about who was moving into Moses Street in the middle of the nineteenth century?

❖ Give reasons for your findings.

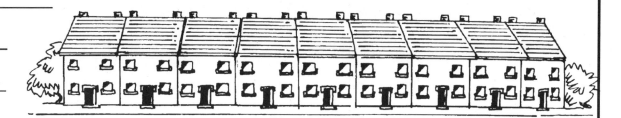

Census returns

Census returns

This is part of a census form.

No. of house-holder's schedule	Name of street, place, or road, and name or No. of house	Name and surname of each person who abode in the house, on the night of the 30th March, 1851	Relation to head of family	Condition	Age of		Rank, profession or occupation	Where born	Whether blind or deaf and dumb
					males	females			
40	Main Street	Hannah Jackson	Head	W		80	Watchmakers widow	Newton	
		William W. D°	Son	Widr	57		Watch and Clock maker	Frodsham	
		William H. D°	Grandson		15		Scholar	Northwich	
		Thomas G. D°	Grandson		13		Apprentice to a watchmaker	Frodsham	

This is what it says:

No. of house-holder's schedule	Name of street, place, or road, and name or No. of house	Name and surname of each person who abode in the house, on the night of the 30th March, 1851	Relation to head of family	Condition	Age of		Rank, profession or occupation	Where born	Whether blind or deaf and dumb
					males	females			
40	Main Street	Hannah Jackson	Head	W		80	Watchmakers widow	Newton	
		William W. D°	Son	Widr	57		Watch and Clock maker	Frodsham	
		William H. D°	Grandson		15		Scholar	Northwich	
		Thomas G. D°	Grandson		13		Apprentice to a watchmaker	Frodsham	

♣ Look at the census form and answer these questions on a piece of paper:

- How many people live in this house?
- Who is the head of the house?

- What are the children's names?
- How old are they?
- What is a scholar?
- What does Widr mean by William's name?

- What other information does the census give us?

♣ Draw a family tree for this household.

Church records

Church wardens' accounts tell how much money is spent on a church and church property.
These are the accounts for a church which were transcribed by a local history society.

The Accounts of the Churchwardens of Lower Molyton
Cecil Clarke & Frederick Littlefield for the year 1679.

April 12th 1680.		
Disbursed by the old Church-Wardens at Easter Visitations.	16 . 2 .	
Bread and Wine at Whitsunday	0 . 2 . 6 .	
at Christmas	0 . 3 . 6 .	
at Easter	0 . 13 . 11 .	
Mowing	0 . 8 .	
Surpless washing	5 . 4 .	
Plumber's work	11 . 4 .	
Glasier his years wages	8 . 0 .	
Wrights work about the roof	1 . 0 .	
Mending the bells and ropes	7 . 10 .	
Smiths work	0 . 11 .	
Bricklayer	5 . 0 .	
Ringers of Christmas	2 . 6 .	

Sum

❖ Why are the accounts not written in Tudor script?

❖ Who was employed by the church during the year 1679?

❖ Which service was best attended? How do you know?

Church registers

Church registers

Church records are often used by people who want to trace their own family tree. What information does this give about members of the Doddsworth family who died between 1790 and 1812?

❖ How many deaths are those of children?

❖ What sort of things did they die from?

❖ What was the main trade undertaken by the adults?

❖ How old was Ralph Doddsworth when he died?

❖ Ask your local vicar if there are any historical documents you could look at, such as Parish registers.

❖ Make a note of any interesting entries.

Date of death	Surname	Christian Name	Name of Parent or Widower	Trade or Profession	Place	Age	Cause of Death
26.7.1811	Dutton	Mary Cecilla	Hugh Hamton	Cotton Mfr		5	Decline
			Frederick				
			Fred				
15.11.1796	Doddsworth	Hannah	Jno		Waterside	3 days	Decline
1.3.1810	Dadsworth	Margaret	James	Weaver	Waterside	1	Decline
19.8.1812	Doddsworth	Martha	John	Weaver	Waterside	¾	Smallpox
10.11.1807	Dadsworth	Mary	John	Weaver	Waterside	1	Whooping Cough
1.5.1811	Dadsworth	Michael	Willm		Waterside	6 mths	Fever
25.1.1800	Doddsworth	Nancy	Willm	Weaver	Waterside	2	Worms
9.11.1792	Doddsworth	Ralph		Soldier	Waterside	96	Old Age
26.8.1802	Dadsworth	Sally	John	Weaver	Waterside	8 wks	Fits
14.8.1795	Doddsworth	Sarah		Widow	Waterside	59	Cancer
2.6.1803	Dadsworth	Sarah	Jas	Weaver	Waterside	14 wks	Fits
3.3.1798	Doddsworth	Susan	John	Weaver	Waterside	20 wks	Decline
10.6.1790	Doddsworth	Susanna			Waterside	Inft	
19.8.1794	Doddsworth	Will	Jno		Waterside	1¾	Smallpox
25.7.1803	Dykes	Amos	Thos	Plasterer	Waterside	1	Whooping Cough

Name _____

Inventories

In many places wills and inventories have survived which tell us about the wealth of individuals. This inventory was found in a local guide book.
'A true and perfect Inventory of all the goods, cattle and chattels of Roger Johnson alias Widowson late of Kirkby in the county of Lancaster husbandman deceased priced period by Edward Woods, Ralph Tyrer, John Leigh and Henry Webster husbandman the second day of November Anno Domini 1638'.

Inprimis	3 horses	viii $l.$
Item	2 carts and 2 ploughs	viii $s.$
Item	in Iron ware for husbandry	li $s.$ vi $d.$
Item	1 brass pot	vi $s.$
Item	in Pewter	ii $s.$
Item	in broken wood in other Implements	x $s.$
Item	the decedent's apparel	xl $s.$
Item	ready money in the decedent's chest	xx $l.$ viii $s.$ vi $d.$

What does it mean?

1. In which year was the inventory made?
2. Whose inventory was it?
3. Where did he live?
4. Who 'priced' the man's goods?
5. How much money did the deceased man (decendent) have in his chest?
6. Why was it not in the bank or building society?
7. What job do you think he had?
8. See if you can find any sort of reference to inventories and wills in local books about your area.
9. What information does it give you about your area?

l = pound s = shilling d = pence

Political pamphlets

Political pamphlets

Pressure groups have often collected data to support their particular cause. This table comes from a pamphlet produced in 1842 which inquired into the living conditions of 5000 families living in one particular Ward in a Victorian City.

		Not Employed	Fully Employed	Employed 5 Days per Week	Employed 4 Days per Week	Employed 3 Days per Week	Employed 2 Days per Week	Employed 1 Day per Week	Not Ascertained	Total
1	Labourers	855	807	17	206	344	271	113	15	2628
2	Widows, and other Females	459	91	2	8	63	56	3	101	783
3	Coopers and Brushmakers	11	31	1	7	9	6	4	–	69
4	Smiths and Engineers	35	89	1	8	14	2	3	5	157
5	Slaters and Plasterers	20	2	1	5	3	5	3	1	40
6	Painters, Plumbers, and Glaziers	28	12	–	6	7	5	6	–	64
7	Joiners and Cabinet-makers	54	48	–	9	5	10	2	26	154
8	Shoe and Boot-makers	50	49	1	23	56	44	18	8	249
9	Tailors	40	24	–	8	30	26	6	4	138
10	Bakers and Millers	10	22	1	–	1	1	–	2	37
11	Bricklayers and Stonemasons	35	11	1	7	9	5	6	1	75
12	Sailors, Fishermen, and Pilots	28	120	–	5	7	3	–	31	194
13	Millwrights and Wheelwrights	5	19	–	2	1	1	1	3	32
14	Engravers and Watchmakers	7	5	–	2	2	4	2	–	22
15	Sawyers	7	8	–	4	6	3	3	6	37
16	Sail-makers, Riggers, and Block-makers	13	12	–	5	10	5	2	–	47
17	Shipwrights and Ropers	16	11	1	10	15	5	2	1	61
18	Printers and Bookbinders	2	8	–	–	1	1	1	11	24
19	Tinmen and Braziers	9	22	–	–	3	1	–	1	36
20	Iron Boiler-makers	6	27	–	3	–	–	–	1	37
21	Iron Moulders	8	12	–	2	–	–	–	–	22
22	Nail-makers	10	16	1	3	2	4	–	–	36
23	Sundry other Trades	29	44	–	1	7	7	1	1	90
		1737	1490	27	324	595	465	176	218	5032

Political pamphlets (continued)

♣ Use the information on the other sheet to complete the following table:

Not employed	
Fully employed	
Employed five days a week	
Employed four days a week	
Employed three days a week	
Employed two days a week	
Employed one day a week	
Not ascertained	
Total	

♣ What do you think the writers of this pamplet wanted to show?

♣ What sort of pamphlets produced in your area might be useful for historians in 100 years time?

Local newspapers

Local newspapers

♣ What information does this give about transport in 1900?

♣ What information does it give about crime prevention?

♣ What information does it give about punishment?

♣ Find a story in your local paper which gives some information which a historian in the future might find useful.

THE WIGAN OBSERVER

Friday April 13, 1900

Wigan Borough Police Court
Thursday
(Before Messrs J Brown, J Gee and R Halliwill)

TRAVELLING WITHOUT A TICKET – Thomas Carton was summoned for travelling on the Lancashire and Yorkshire Railway from Preston Road to Wigan without a ticket, with intent to avoid payment thereof. – Mr J Peck prosecuted – The evidence showed that on the 27th March defendant was seen to travel from Preston Road to Wigan and when he reached Wigan he went to the ticket office and bought a ticket for Orrell. At the barrier he was asked for a ticket and he then said he had only been in the refreshment room. The collector, from information received, went after him, and asked him for his name and address. Defendant said he had not enough money and went to borrow some.

A fine of 10s and costs was imposed, and he was ordered to pay the fare 1s. $3\frac{1}{2}$d.

Name _____

Street directory

❖ Match the names in the directory to the houses.

Glwadys Street

1 Wood, Mrs. Eleanor

3 Osborne, William Herbert

5 Ely, Joseph

7 Evans, Mrs. Catherine

❖ Make a street directory for your home and neighbours.

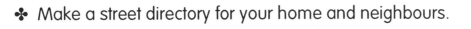

Street plan

Street plan

❖ Put a circle round the shops which were in Church Street in both 1932 and 1958.

❖ On a piece of paper draw the street as it might have looked in 1932.

❖ On another piece of paper draw the street as it might have looked in 1958.

Church Street 1932

CHURCH ST. (1)

2 Whitechapel

LEFT SIDE

1 & 3 BUNNEY'S LIMITED,
household stores, ladies'
wear, sports, toys and
presentation goods importers

5 Beaverbrooks jewellers
7 Russell-Douglas ophthalmic opticns
7 Guinea Dress Shop Ltd

**9 to 15 HENDERSON WM. &
SONS LTD,** silk mercers
and general drapers
TEL. No. Royal 4848 (5 lines)

Williamson St

17 Lloyds Bank Ltd
19 Peacock S.G. Ltd advertisers' agts
19 Studio Sefton commrcl. artists
19 Smith Miss Laura, M.I.S.Ch., S.R.N.,
    C.S.M.M.G. masseuse
19 Beveridge & Holt ladies' hairdrssrs
19 Petty & Sons (Leeds) Ltd, printers
21 Kardomah Exhibition Café
23 Ciro Pearls, Ltd. jewellers
25 Joan's Fashion Shop gowns
27 Trace W.H. & Son electricians
25 Capital & Provincial News Theatres Ltd

**29 SCHIERWATER &
LLOYD LTD.** jewellers &
agents for the Waltham Watch Co.

31 Barker & Dobson, Ltd. confctnrs

Tarleton St

33 Saxone Shoe Co. Ltd. boot mkrs
35 Maison Lyons (J. Lyons & Co. Ltd.)
    café restaurant
    Marks & Spencer departmental store
    'Compton House'

43 BELL & CO. gown & blouse
specialists

45 Swears & Wells Ltd. furriers

Church Street 1958

CHURCH ST. (1)

2 Whitechapel

LEFT SIDE

1 & 3 Greenwoods (H. & O.) Ltd. outfitters
5 Tyler Jn. & Sons Ltd. footwear specialists
7 Paige Gowns Ltd. costumiers

**9 to 15 HENDERSON WM. &
SONS Ltd.** fashion specialists
and general drapers
Tel. No. Royal 6441 (10 lines)

Williamson St

21 Kardomah Café
23 Bewlay & Co. Ltd. tobccnsts
25 'Tatler', Capital & Provincial News
    Theatres Ltd
25 & 25A Milletts Stores (1928) Ltd. outfitters
27 & 29 Samuel H. Ltd. jewellers
31 Barker & Dobson Ltd. confctnrs

Tarleton St

33 Saxone Shoe Co. Ltd. boot mkrs
35 Maison Lyons (J. Lyons & Co. Ltd.)
    café restaurant
    Marks & Spencer Ltd. departmental store
    'Compton House'
45 Swears & Wells Ltd. furriers

Picture prompts

✤ Choose an old photograph and look at it carefully.

✤ Look for clues to help you answer the questions opposite.

✤ Look at the people and how they are dressed. What else can you see in the background?

✤ How would it be different if the photograph was taken today?

Now fill in your answers

✤ What can you see in the picture? _____

_____

_____

✤ Where do you think the photograph was taken? _____

_____

_____

✤ When do you think it was taken? _____

_____

_____

✤ Why do you think it was taken? _____

_____

_____

✤ What's your evidence for this? _____

_____

_____

Interpreting photographs

Photograph of: _____

Year taken (if known): _____

Who might have taken the photograph? _____

What do you think happened after the photograph was taken? _____

Is it posed or natural? _____

Why I think the photograph was taken: _____

Do you have any other sources of evidence about the photograph? _____

✤ Place the photograph in the middle of a large sheet of paper. Extend the picture by drawing the scene all around it.

Above ground clues – fact sheet

Above ground clues – fact sheet

Aerial photographs provide useful evidence about what has happened in the very distant past.

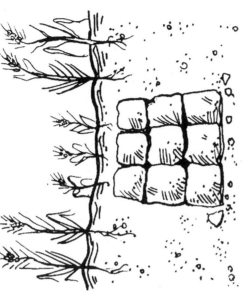

Crops come up later and fade earlier where they grow above ancient walls.

Crops come up earlier and stay greener where there are ancient pits filled with soil.

Faint ground markings visible only from the air indicate places where buildings once stood.

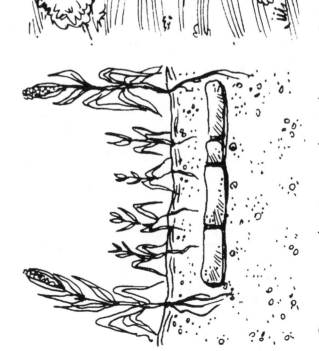

Corn grows shorter over buried road surfaces or ancient walls.

Name _____

Memories: which is which?

Memories: which is which?

My grandmother was in service. She used to tell me how she had to get up at 5 o'clock each morning and clean the fires.

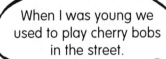

I went to Disneyland this summer and saw Mickey Mouse.

When I was young we used to play cherry bobs in the street.

♣ Which is the eye-witness account?

♣ Which is the hearsay?

♣ Which one is a reminiscence?

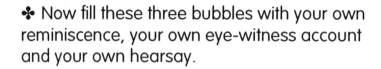

♣ Now fill these three bubbles with your own reminiscence, your own eye-witness account and your own hearsay.

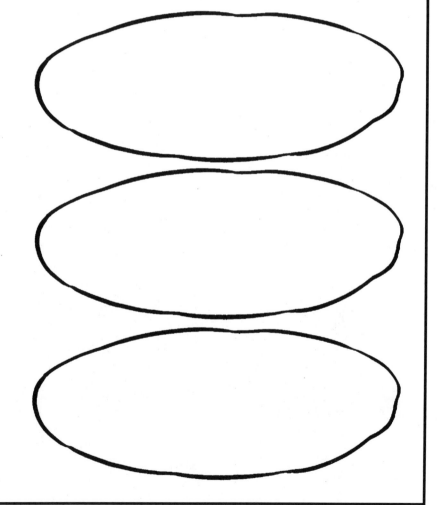

Badges

Do you know which war these badges came from?

♣ Find someone who has them and ask them about how they won them.

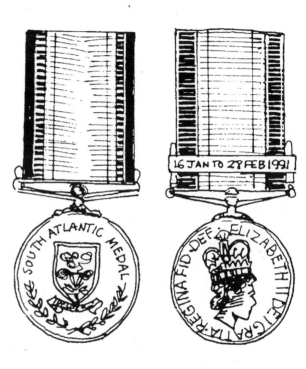

Farming interview

Farming interview

Address of Farm: _____

Type of Farm: _____

Date of visit: _____

❖ How long have you worked on the farm? _____

❖ What sort of work do you do? _____

❖ How many other people work here? _____

❖ What work do they do? _____

❖ Can you describe a typical day's routine? _____

❖ Do you work on the farm every day of the week? _____

❖ What sort of holidays do you get? _____

❖ What things have changed since you first started working as a farmer? _____

Oral evidence: school in the past

Oral evidence: school in the past

Name(s) of interviewer: _____

Name of interviewee: _____

Age of interviewee: _____

Date of interview: _____

Question	Answer
How many schools did you attend?	
What were they called?	
How old were you when you left school?	
How many children were in your class at primary school?	
Did you have milk or dinners at school?	
How did the teachers punish you?	
What lessons did you have?	
What was your favourite lesson?	
How did you get to school?	
What important events do you remember while you were at school?	
What do you think has changed most since you were at school?	

Name _____

General interview

Name of interviewer: _____

Name of interviewee: _____

Date of interview: _____

Subject of interview: _____

Question 1 _____

Question 2 _____

Question 3 _____

Question 4 _____

Additional information _____

_____

_____

_____

_____